HERBARIUM

CAZ HILDEBRAND

Thames & Hudson

Contents

Introduction

This is a book of herbs. There are sweet herbs – basil, angelica, pandan – and tart herbs – sorrel, bergamot, sassafras. There are minty herbs and oniony herbs and bitter herbs. There are tall herbs that whisper, and small herbs that shout. There are herbs to eat and herbs very much not to eat; some of them heal, but there are a few that could kill. Not all herbs are green, although there are a lot of green herbs.

WE'RE MISSING OUT on herbs if we don't appreciate their multi-dimensional personalities: their varyingly medicinal, culinary, spiritual, cultural and magical qualities and histories. They are all fascinating, each with their own stories to tell; I've very much wanted to listen to each herb, to let it speak for itself. Where flowers bring beauty to the garden, herbs bring that but also usefulness, morality, wisdom.

In his *Herbal of All Sorts* (1959), the poet and naturalist Geoffrey Grigson reminds us that herbs once belonged to 'Plant Time' – 'when plants were supremely important in day-to-day life (for more than food) and were believed to contain souls or spirits, so that many plants had to be treated with respect, and picked with caution'. So revered were herbs that they had to be picked by the 'silveriest light of the full moon'; some herbalists even walked backwards to the plant – to surprise it. The more naked (or at least barefooted) the picker, the better. Like Grigson, I'm more inclined – with my clothes on – 'to pounce towards the plant'. It has been a glorious enterprise to hold, be with, stroke, feel, sniff, taste and otherwise research each and every herb – all 100 of them – in this book.

What is a herb? Definitions vary, of course, but the simplest could go something like this: herbs are plants that are useful to humans for flavouring, food, medicine or perfume. It is helpful, perhaps, to distinguish herbs from spices: we might think of the herb as the fresh, leafier part of a plant, whereas the spice is the dried seed, berry or root – although that is by no means a rule. Herbs are generally used in small amounts, but not always – tabbouleh, for example, is dominated by parsley. In many cases, herbs are simply weeds in the right place at the right time.

This volume comes in a long tradition of books that combine words and illustrations to illuminate the beauty and the uses of herbaceous plants. Herbals – from the medieval Latin *liber herbalis*, meaning 'book of herbs' – were some of the first books produced in ancient civilizations and contained the latest and best medical knowledge available to herbalists and apothecaries. In Europe, herbals flourished for 200 years after the introduction of moveable type at the end of the fifteenth century. One of the earliest printed herbals with woodcut illustrations was Konrad von Megenberg's *Buch der Natur* in 1475.

The famous English herbalists John Gerard (1542–1612) and Nicholas Culpeper (1616–1654) have been particularly inspiring to me. Of course, these herbalists on the cusp of the Enlightenment worked in turn with their own heritage herbals, those from the classical world – Dioscorides' *De Materia Medica* and Pliny's *Naturalis Historia* – not to mention keeping their own herb gardens and treating patients for every ailment under the sun.

In this book, the ambition from the start was to illustrate the herbs in such a way as to form a set of elements that created beautiful patterns. The way we have designed the herbs echoes the history of herbal illustration, but with the intention of taking it forward, achieved by using a contemporary style, inspired by Modernist design, simple geometric forms and vibrant colours. I love the patterns that come through – look at chives (page 23), pandan (page 148) and salad burnet (page 179), for example – and hope you do too.

Now that ever more arcane herbs are available in supermarkets and nurseries, and our tastes are becoming increasingly cosmopolitan, we can benefit from a fuller understanding of the power of herbs to flavour our food, heal our ills, scent our homes and restore our spirits. In thinking about herbs, it is clear that they have always had an essential part to play in culinary, medical and spiritual aspects of life. Encouraging their appropriate use – with justified appreciation for their beauty – is the purpose of this book.

CAZ HILDEBRAND

The Herbs

English Mace

*Not to be confused with the spice, which is the outer husk
of nutmeg, nor assumed to be English (it's actually Swiss),
English mace deserves much more popularity in its own right
than its misleading name seems to allow.*

GROW
Take cuttings in late summer
and, once rooted, plant out
in the garden 30 cm (12 in.)
apart. It grows well in large
pots, too.

EAT WITH
Chicken, fish, fennel,
cauliflower, asparagus,
potatoes, beans, rice, pasta,
plums, peaches.

TRY
Make a tisane of English
mace leaves by infusing a
small clump in boiled water
for five minutes, sweetening
to taste. Add a few young
leaves to a green salad or
a potato salad, or try adding
them to sorbets and ice
creams.

HEAL
A tisane of English mace may
alleviate the symptoms of
the common cold.

A COUSIN OF YARROW (see page 12), and also known as sweet Nancy, English mace was discovered in Switzerland in 1798 and is now cultivated in many temperate northern areas. Its bright green foliage is suited to windier positions, given that the stems are strong and tall. Each one carries many daisy-like flowers, which are long-lived and bloom well into autumn.

It is remarkable that this dainty delight has associations with powerful Achilles, the Greek hero of the Trojan War. The genus is thought to be named after him because he discovered its medicinal properties – properties that are deemed obsolete now, although a cup of English mace tea is said to help cure a cold.

The frilly, hairy, aromatic leaves can be used when young to flavour soups, stews, potato salad, rice, pasta and chicken dishes, although they should be added sparingly lest they overpower the other ingredients. In summer, pick bunches of the stems and hang them upside down to dry before using them in dried-flower arrangements.

Achillea millefolium

Yarrow

About 60,000 years ago, a man was buried in a tomb in what is now Iraq with spring flowers that included yarrow; all the flowers had health benefits, suggesting that he was a Shanidar medicine man.

GROW
Yarrow likes to grow in full sun. Sow seed indoors eight weeks before the last frost is expected. Once planted, it needs little care. Grow in the garden or in pots.

EAT WITH
Fish, seafood, chicken, peaches, plums, lettuce, beetroot.

TRY
Add finely chopped young yarrow leaves to green salads, being sure to include some milder herbs to offset the bitterness.

HEAL
Some people notice relief from allergy symptoms by drinking yarrow and mint tisane. An external tincture or poultice can help haemorrhoids, rashes and broken skin. Yarrow can be used for indigestion and loss of appetite, and to treat fevers. Use in pillows, sleep tinctures and oil to promote relaxation. Pregnant women and children should not use it.

A ROADSIDE AND PASTURELAND plant common throughout Europe, Asia and North America, yarrow is an ancient herb. Its Latin name derives partly from Achilles, who is said to have healed many of his warriors with haemorrhage-controlling yarrow leaves, not least himself (although, alas, famously not his heel). A long-stemmed member of the sunflower family, yarrow can be recognized by its highly segmented leaves: *millefolium* means 'a thousand leaves', and thousand leaf is another of its common names.

With lacy white and yellow flowers that sway gently in the breeze (their scent is sweet and liquoricey, and they taste a little like cardamom), yarrow is sometimes called carpenter's herb: it's good at healing wounds. One of its other names is nosebleed, since it was used in the nineteenth century both to treat and to cause them. Indeed, yarrow became associated with testing a lover's faithfulness: the herb was pushed up the lover's nose and rotated several times – if the lover was faithful, the enquirer's nose would bleed.

Yarrow has a sweet taste with bitter afternotes that can be overpowering. Cooking seems to bring out its bitterness. Conversely, the sweetness of the raw herb works well with fruit and in creamy desserts. The flowers are a key ingredient of heather beer, a homemade beer based on wild ingredients including hops, honey, seaweed and heather twigs.

Monkshood

*Extremely poisonous, monkshood – or wolf's bane, as it is
also known – is a herbaceous perennial that is chiefly native
to the mountainous parts of the northern hemisphere.*

GROW
Beautiful to look at, this
poisonous plant should
be grown where it is not
accessible. Plant it at the
back of borders or under
trees, and avoid it entirely
if your garden is frequented
by children or pets.

INCLUDED HERE TO demonstrate the darker arts, monkshood is
highly toxic. As with many herbs, there is a great deal in the name:
monkshood because the tall stem bears flowers whose sepals are in
the form of a cylindrical helmet, looking not unlike a monk's cowl;
and wolf's bane because the toxins were once extracted from the
plant and used to kill wolves. The herb has long been associated
with big dogs, and the classical writer Ovid has it in the slavering
mouth of three-headed Cerberus, guard dog to the gates of hell.
Aconitum is Greek for 'dart', because the juice was used to poison
arrow tips. *Napellus*, or 'little turnip', is a reference to the shape of
its roots.

In her *Modern Herbal* (1931), Mrs Grieve goes to great pains
to describe the considerable agonies of being poisoned with
monkshood: 'tingling and numbness of tongue and mouth and a
sensation of ants crawling over the body, nausea and vomiting with
epigastric pain, laboured breathing, pulse irregular and weak, skin
cold and clammy, features bloodless, giddiness, staggering, mind
remains clear'. No joking around, then: monkshood is a herb
to avoid. It can be used as an ingredient to soothe the pains of
neuralgia, sciatica, arthritis, gout, measles and chronic skin problems,
but it is definitely one to leave to the professional herbalists.

Agastache foeniculum

Anise Hyssop

———

With their spiky flowers and spicily scented leaves, the hitherto under-appreciated agastaches are making a comeback.

GROW
Anise hyssop is easy to grow from seed: either start it indoors or sow outside in spring or autumn. It loves sunny spots and partial shade alike, and thrives in well-drained garden soil.

EAT WITH
Chicken, pork, lamb, fish, green beans, root vegetables, tomatoes, raspberries, strawberries, blackberries, apricots, peaches, plums.

TRY
Add finely chopped anise hyssop flowers to the dough when making shortbread. Make hyssop sugar by adding a few flowers to a jar of caster (superfine) sugar and leaving to infuse. Add to marinades for fish, chicken and pork. Infuse flowers in boiling water to make a tisane that is reputedly good for hangovers.

HEAL
The antibacterial leaves, infused, can alleviate the symptoms of coughs and colds. They can be used as a compress to soothe fevers and headaches. Add to foot baths to treat athlete's foot.

THE LEAVES AND tiny flowers (forming long purple spikes) of probably the best known agastache, anise hyssop, smell and taste of anise and fennel, although its stems and large-textured leaves show that it is in fact a member of the mint family. Funnily enough, anise hyssop, which is native to North America, is no relation to either anise or hyssop, and is indeed sometimes called liquorice mint. The upright, short-lived perennial can grow to over 1 m (3 ft) tall, with long, bottlebrush spikes of purple, blue and pink flowers that are attractive to bees.

There are plenty of other agastaches, each with its own scent and flavour, including the fragrant and extremely pretty Mexican hyssop (*Agastache mexicana*) and the spearmint- and liquorice-scented Korean mint (*A. rugosa*), a deciduous perennial native to eastern Asia, with big, rough, serrated leaves. For their colour and like-minded temperament, agastaches grow well with Japanese anemones and white ornamentals such as campanulas, or with chives, oregano and thyme.

Alchemilla vulgaris

Lady's Mantle

_Growing no taller than 30 cm (12 in.), lady's mantle
is a herbaceous perennial that produces a mass of tiny,
yellow-green flowers and leaves that are rounded like the
edge of a cloak._

GROW
A self-seeder, lady's mantle
can be grown outdoors
from seed after the last
frost, or sown indoors and
transplanted.

TRY
Make a tisane by pouring
a cup of boiled water onto
two teaspoons of dried lady's
mantle and leaving it to
infuse for up to ten minutes.

HEAL
Used in skin lotion, lady's
mantle can help with eczema,
cuts, wounds, sores and
insect bites. A decoction
can also be gargled as
a mouthwash to treat
ulcers, bleeding gums
and sore throats.

T HAT IS WHERE its name comes from – but this is not just
anyone's mantle. The herb was much admired by the Christian
Church (it called it a 'woman's best friend'), and the lady in question
is, of course, the Virgin Mary. As with many herbs that seem
designed especially for women – the ones the astrological herbalist
Nicholas Culpeper described as coming 'under Venus' – its reputed
ability to help with menstrual problems, pregnancy and breast-
related ailments is associated with the mother of Jesus. Historically,
the herb has been used for what we now call post-natal depression.
The deep cup of the leaves makes them perfect for holding water
droplets, and the dew thus collected has in the past been associated
with magical qualities.

Interestingly, it's not just for matters of the female body that
lady's mantle allegedly works wonders: it is also associated with
gentleness, elegance and grace, coupled with power and authority.
And, despite its association with female ailments, it was also used
by soldiers in the fifteenth and sixteenth centuries to staunch
bloody wounds on the battlefield, as Culpeper explained in his
Herbal. Slightly old-fashioned these days, lady's mantle grows in
North America, Europe, Iceland, Asia and Siberia, and has always
been associated with healing properties – hence the Arab *alkemelych*
(alchemy) in its botanical name.

Garlic

*'Eat no onions nor garlic, for we are to utter sweet breath,
and I do not doubt but hear them say, it is a sweet comedy.'*

WILLIAM SHAKESPEARE, A MIDSUMMER NIGHT'S DREAM

GROW
Propagate this hardy perennial or biennial by planting cloves in rich, moist soil in plenty of sunshine.

EAT WITH
Pretty much any savoury ingredient benefits from the addition of garlic.

TRY
Don't forget the retro joys of garlic bread. Mash four crushed garlic cloves (and some chopped herbs, if you like) into 130 g (4½ oz) butter. Make incisions all the way along a baguette, being careful not to cut through the base. Insert lavish amounts of the butter, then wrap in foil and bake in a hot oven for about fifteen minutes, until the butter has melted and the bread is crisp on the outside.

HEAL
Garlic is used to help prevent heart disease, high cholesterol and high blood pressure, and to boost the immune system. It can be taken in supplements or as raw cloves with meals.

HALITOSIS NOTWITHSTANDING, GARLIC has long been associated with protection and with the warding off of unhelpful things like vampires, demons and werewolves; it was hung from windows and rubbed into chimneys and keyholes. The Romans, like the Greeks, valued garlic for the strength it gave their soldiers, something the Indian poet Sujata Bhatt writes about in *The Stinking Rose* (1995), a collection of poems devoted to it. Research suggests that allicin, an amino acid present in garlic, can reduce cholesterol levels, lower blood pressure and help to prevent the common cold.

Pungent and hot when dried, which is the way it is usually sold, garlic is much milder when green and fresh, a form that is sometimes described as wet garlic. In the Mediterranean raw garlic is celebrated the most: crushed in salad dressings; pounded with egg yolks and oil to make the Provençal sauce aioli; beaten into mashed potato or bread with olive oil and lemon juice for the Greek dip skordalia; or finely chopped with parsley to make the French persillade, or with parsley and lemon for the Italian gremolata. For a subtler, but still pervasive, flavour, garlic is finely sliced or chopped and fried in oil. Roasting the bulb whole brings out its sweetness, reducing the flesh to a soft, sticky paste. The longer the cooking and the less the cloves are broken down, the mellower the taste, as the infamous French recipe for chicken with forty garlic cloves attests. The erudite chef Stevie Parle is brief about one of his favourite ingredients: 'Garlic is amazing.' Given all the ways garlic can be used – for sweetness or bitterness, sliced or crushed – he adds, 'I seem to be constantly learning.'

Allium schoenoprasum

Chives

The famous herbalist Nicholas Culpeper had to confess that he had accidentally omitted chives from the first edition of his seventeenth-century herbal encyclopedia.

GROW
Chives are easy to grow, but do water them regularly, because the roots stay near the surface. Cut rather than pull them and they'll reappear next spring.

EAT WITH
Avocados, potatoes, tomatoes, beetroot, fish, seafood, eggs, smoked fish, cheese.

TRY
Chives go famously well with baked potatoes, stirred into thick yogurt to accompany grilled fish or sprinkled on scrambled eggs. Celebrate the whole plant by pickling the chive bulblets in vinegar to accompany pâtés and cold meats.

HEAL
The allicin in chives is connected to lowering blood pressure. Quercetin – also found in chives – can help to lower the risk of stroke and heart attack. Chives are very versatile: they can help with digestive problems, maintain bone health and strengthen the immune system.

IT WAS THANKS to a 'country gentleman' who spotted this anomaly that Culpeper added 'cives' to the next book. Perhaps he'd forgotten to include the allium for a reason; he confesses that they 'cause troublesome sleep and spoil the eyesight'.

Also known as rush leeks, chives were thought by the Romans to relieve sunburn and sore throats. Having grown wild across Europe and North America, they began to be cultivated properly in the Middle Ages, and became popular in the nineteenth century. No surprise, perhaps: they are high in vitamin C, potassium and folic acid, and are known to promote good digestion and prevent bad breath.

The smallest member of the lily family (and a close relative of the onion), long, green, grass-like chives are delicately flavoured, adding a mildly oniony bite to savoury dishes. They are simple to prepare, too: just snip with scissors. If you are doing this straight from the plant, cut from about 5 cm (2 in.) from the ground to encourage the plant to grow tall. Always add your snipped chives at the end of cooking to prevent loss of flavour. The lavender-coloured flowers can also be eaten: add them to salads for a subtler chive flavour.

Ramsons

————

A favourite leaf of brown bears (a fact that gives the herb both its Latin name and its nickname, bear leek), ramsons – or wild garlic – are native to Europe and Asia and a close relative of chives.

GROW
If you cannot find ramsons growing wild, sow from seed – they are easy to grow in fertile, well-drained soil with plenty of shade. Bear in mind that they are invasive, though.

EAT WITH
Asparagus, mushrooms, eggs, potatoes, pasta, rice, cheese, fish, seafood, lamb, chicken, pork.

TRY
Season cleaned, gutted fish, such as trout, red mullet or small sea bass, and wrap each one in ramsons and then in foil. Cook on a barbecue for about twenty-five minutes, turning halfway through.

HEAL
Ramsons are antibacterial, antibiotic and antiseptic and can help to reduce blood pressure and the risk of heart attack and stroke. Pile them into your diet when you can.

THERE IS NOTHING quite like coming across swathes of wild garlic on a cool, damp woodland walk – and it will be your nose that discovers them first. Ramsons are a must to harvest in late spring and early summer. Their elegant, pointed leaves have a sweetness and sharpness, both in taste and aroma, that is reminiscent of chives and spring onions (scallions) – and of garlic itself, of course. The delicate white flowers are edible too, although the leaves taste best before the plants flower. Wild garlic has been beneficial to humans for centuries, and seemingly has more health benefits than bulb garlic (see page 20). Compounds in the herb can promote general bodily health, reducing blood pressure and cholesterol levels. A hint for foragers: look for ramsons on slopes, since they will have had less animal traffic. Be aware that although ramsons are completely edible, some of their lookalikes are not, including lily of the valley (page 66) and snowdrops. To check that you have indeed found your wild allium, break a leaf and sniff it for garlic pungency. Be sure to wash the leaves well before use.

Don't pass up the chance to take advantage of ramsons in the kitchen during their short season. Despite their strong scent, they are surprisingly mild in flavour, making them an excellent way to imbue your cooking with a subtle garlicky note. Try them shredded and added to omelettes, frittatas, scrambled eggs and risottos. You can also add them to soups (at the last minute, for maximum flavour), or substitute them for basil to make a really punchy pesto. Blanched in boiling water, then drained and puréed, ramsons make a lovely base for homemade mayonnaise.

Lemon Verbena

*For everything from lemon ices to soothing tea and summer
cocktails, lemon verbena – originally from Chile and Peru –
is the next best thing to growing your own lemon tree.*

GROW

It's best to grow lemon verbena in a pot so that it can be taken indoors in the winter – it doesn't like frost. Regular trimming will keep your verbena bushy. Do not be taken aback if it drops its leaves; the shedding does not mean it is dead.

EAT WITH

Strawberries, apricots, peaches, carrots, mushrooms, rice, chicken, fish.

TRY

Add sprigs of lemon verbena to the pan when making apricot, peach or strawberry jam. Include lots of chopped verbena in a rice salad with finely sliced dried apricots, gentle spices such as coriander and cinnamon, and toasted pine nuts.

HEAL

Lemon verbena tea has soothing qualities and can alleviate stomach problems such as cramping and bloating. Drunk before exercise, it has even been shown to decrease damage to muscles during a workout.

LACKING THE SOURNESS of lemon, while maximizing the citrus flavour, lemon verbena has an intoxicatingly fresh, pure lemon fragrance; the Spanish cultivated it for perfumes. In *Gone with the Wind*, it is Scarlett O'Hara's mother's favourite scent. As well as having a beautiful aroma, lemon verbena can boost the immune system, ease stress and fortify the nervous system.

Lemon verbena can be used in cooking whenever you want a fresh, lemony taste: with chicken and fish, in sauces, dips and salads, and with fruit and all manner of desserts. Verbena ices are a refreshing summer treat: pour 500 ml (17 fl. oz) boiling water over a handful of crushed lemon verbena sprigs and 4 tablespoons of sugar and leave to cool, then chill. Strain, pour into ice-lolly moulds and freeze.

Lemon verbena sprigs are also delightful muddled in a fragrant gin and tonic or infused in boiling water to make one of the best and most soothing herbal teas. A combination of lemon verbena and mint works well in tea, too. If you have a lot of lemon verbena, dry it in the oven on the lowest setting and use it in potpourri, linen sachets and herb cushions.

Marsh Mallow

Not quite the squidgy cuboid toasted over the bonfire (although that was originally flavoured by its roots), the African marsh mallow plant has been used as a food and medicine for more than 2,000 years.

GROW

A slow grower, this one: sow in autumn in trays and winter outside under glass. In spring, when the seedlings are large enough, plant them out, leaving 45 cm (18 in.) between them. Marsh mallow will flower in the second year, but it will be a few years before the roots can be harvested.

TRY

The Romans considered marsh mallow a beautiful vegetable, and stuffed suckling pigs with it. If you're short of a pig, you can simply boil marsh mallow roots until soft, then peel them and fry in butter.

HEAL

The roots and leaves are most commonly used in tinctures, capsules and tea. Tinctures can alleviate sore throats and dry coughs. The tea works well for indigestion. Capsules can be used to alleviate Crohn's disease.

COMMONLY FOUND NEAR the sea, marsh mallow stands tall and proud in salty soil, its thick, fleshy, upright stems reaching heights of over 1 m (3 ft) tall. The tapered, pale yellow roots are long, tough and thick, with a flexible exterior; they were eaten regularly before the potato ploughed its way into our diet. The round, fuzzy leaves have jagged margins and three to five lobes, which are almost the shape of Africa if you squint (a strange coincidence, given its origin). They are soft to the touch, thanks to a covering of velvety down. Marsh mallow's pleasing flowers are mostly white with hints of red, and they do a lot of good work attracting bees.

Althaea comes from the Latin for 'I cure'. It is the high dosage of mucilage throughout the plant, and especially in the root, that makes marsh mallow so useful to herbalists and their patients. Recent studies have shown that it can soothe irritated mucous membranes, bronchitis, sore throats and coughs, indigestion and skin inflammation. Dried leaves may be used in infusions and tinctures. The roots are used dried in extracts, capsules, ointments, creams and cough syrups.

Anethum graveolens

Dill

Dill – a member of the parsley family and a not-too-distant relation of fennel – is indigenous to western Asia, although it is now cultivated all over the world.

GROW
Sow this self-seeding annual in rich soil, sheltered from strong winds. Plant it next to cabbages or onions, but keep it away from carrots – dill produces root excretions that are harmful to them.

EAT WITH
Smoked fish, seafood, lamb, beef, mushrooms, broad (fava) beans, beetroot, carrots, cabbage, cucumber, potatoes, rice, soured cream, yogurt, eggs, paprika.

TRY
Make dill butter: beat plenty of chopped dill and a little lemon zest and juice into softened butter, shape into a log, then wrap in foil and chill. Slice and serve on steak, lamb chops, fish or vegetables.

HEAL
Bring vitamin A- and C-rich dill into your diet to help with insomnia, hiccoughs, diarrhoea and menstrual and respiratory disorders. It can be a powerful boost to the immune system and is anti-inflammatory, so can protect against arthritis.

THIS DELICATE HERB is much loved in many countries. In Serbia, 'to be a dill in every soup' corresponds to the English saying 'to have a finger in every pie'. In the Azores, dill is the most important ingredient in the most important dish, Holy Ghost soup. In German folklore, brides put dill and salt in their shoes for luck.

The name comes from the Norse *dilla*, meaning 'lull', and dill certainly has a reputation for being soothing: the herb is an important component of gripe water, invented by William Woodward in the nineteenth century to 'soothe fretful babies and [provide] relief from gastrointestinal troubles in infants'. The Greek philosopher Pythagoras taught that holding dill in one's left hand helped to prevent epilepsy.

Identifiable by its feathery leaves and soft, sweet, citrusy taste, dill is an essential ingredient in Russia, Scandinavia and central and eastern Europe. It goes well with salmon, crab and scallops, and is at its best in the Scandinavian gravadlax, but it is also good with many vegetables and works surprisingly well with other herbs, such as mint, basil and parsley. The Scandinavians infuse vodka with dill, while in Turkey and Greece it is added to soups, dips and egg dishes. In central European countries it is used in pickles – and, of course, it also appears in the famous kosher dill pickle of Jewish delicatessens.

The fourth-century Roman cookery book *De re coquinaria* – 'The Art of Cooking' – has a recipe for flamingo stew, which involves parboiling the pink wading bird in salty water and plenty of dill. Dates and leeks are added and the pepper mill twisted, before 'covering the bird with sauce' and serving. As if killing two birds with one recipe: 'Parrot is prepared in the same manner.'

Angelica

Preferring to grow in damp, lightly shaded places, angelica is a giant of the herb world and, given that it can grow to such heights, also of the garden.

GROW
Plant angelica seeds in rich soil in shade. Staking is wise in more exposed areas, given the plant's height. Cut back after flowering.

EAT WITH
Strawberries, raspberries, gooseberries, rhubarb, apples, plums, lemon.

TRY
Cook chopped angelica leaves or stalks with rhubarb, gooseberries, plums or apples; you won't need so much sugar, as the angelica counters the acidity of the fruit. Macerate rhubarb or strawberries with sugar and chopped angelica leaves or stalks before making jam. Boil young angelica stalks, toss with butter and serve as a vegetable.

HEAL
Angelica essential oil is used to relax nerves and muscles. With vapour therapy, it can help with bronchitis and asthma; added to bathwater it can aid the lymphatic system and fight fungal growth; and in creams it can help with poor circulation, arthritis, migraines, colds and flu.

THIS AROMATIC PERENNIAL herb of great height and structure – it grows an impressive 2 m (6 ft) tall – bears white or pale yellow flowers that protrude in rounded umbels (or clusters) from hollow stems. Its name comes from the Greek word *angelos*, meaning 'messenger' (as in herald of good news), because the fourteenth-century physician Mattheus Sylvaticus reportedly had a dream that angelica could cure the plague (and indeed, angelica was used as a plague curative in England until the time of Charles II). The whole herb is aromatic, with a sweet, musky scent when rubbed, and the flowers have a honeyed fragrance.

This 'angel-like herb' (Nicholas Culpeper) has been used to treat everything from indigestion and anaemia to coughs and colds. The Aleut people of Alaska traditionally applied the boiled roots of angelica to wounds to speed up healing. Spiritually, angelica has been used to promote the protection of the home and to fend off evil, including witches. Less spiritually, its crushed leaves can act as an air freshener. Angelica is often sold candied as a decoration for desserts and cakes. The fresh herb can be used to infuse milk-based desserts, such as custards and ice creams, or added to jams.

Anthriscus cerefolium

Chervil

---

*'Chervill is used very much among the Dutch people in a kind
of Loblolly or Hotchpot which they do eat, called Warmus.'*

JOHN GERARD, HERBALL, OR, GENERALL HISTORIE
OF PLANTES, 1597

GROW
Chervil needs a moist spot
in dappled shade. It grows
quickly; you'll be harvesting
it six to eight weeks after
sowing. Cut outer leaves first,
to encourage new growth at
the centre of the plant.

EAT WITH
Beetroot, asparagus,
carrots, cauliflower, lettuce,
mushrooms, fennel, potatoes,
tomatoes, lemon, chicken,
veal, white fish, soft cheese,
eggs.

TRY
Sprinkle chopped chervil over
roasted fennel to accentuate
the aniseed flavour. Dress
hot potatoes with a chervil
vinaigrette. Stir chopped
chervil into mayonnaise to
accompany fish or chicken.
Fold a handful of chervil
through hot, buttered peas.

HEAL
Choose chervil for lagging
vigour and low spirits. Being
rich in iron, calcium and
magnesium, chervil can
promote the production
of blood and the healthy
function of nerves and
muscles.

CHEERFUL CHERVIL – the name derives from the Greek
chaerophyllon, meaning 'herb of rejoicing' – is a sparer, more feathery,
curly parsley lookalike. Gerard added: 'It is good for old people:
it rejoiceth and comforteth the heart and increaseth their strength.'
And it is true to say that in European folklore, eating the happy
herb was encouraged not only to aid digestion but also to foster
cheerfulness and a sharp wit.

This delicately aniseed-flavoured herb can be hard to find
in shops, although it is easy to cultivate in the garden or on a
windowsill. And there's much to be cheerful about when you
do get your hands on it: it is a versatile herb that deserves more
experimentation. The French seem to appreciate it most. It is an
essential component of that great French tradition *fines herbes*, along
with parsley, chives and tarragon; it is often added to béarnaise
sauce; and it is used in sauces for fish and chicken. A smattering
of chervil leaves is routinely added to egg dishes, such as omelettes,
quiches, scrambled eggs and *oeufs en cocotte*. In Holland, a favourite
early autumn soup, *kelleversop*, is made with chervil, potatoes, shallots,
cream and egg yolks. A member of the carrot family, chervil also
goes extremely well with carrots, either as a garnish or in a soup
or salad.

Édouard de Pomiane, in his classic *Cooking with Pomiane* (1930),
which helped to revolutionize classic French cuisine, recommended
chopped chervil with cucumber and cream: 'It is delicious.'

Celery

———

Grown for its leaves rather than its stalks, herb celery – also known as leaf celery or smallage – has a parsley-like aroma with a pleasingly bitter taste.

GROW
Grow celery from seed in soil that retains moisture, and water frequently. You'll get your reward throughout summer and winter, although watch out for slugs.

EAT WITH
Chicken, pork, lamb, beef, game, fish, blue cheese, apples, nuts, cabbage, tomatoes, onions, potatoes, rice.

TRY
Add chopped celery leaf to potato or bean salads. Mix with tuna and mayonnaise for a sandwich filling. Cook celery leaf in a tomato sauce to serve with pasta. Stir finely sliced celery leaf into celeriac rémoulade.

HEAL
Celery leaf can reduce blood pressure – it contains pthalides, which can lower the level of stress hormones in the blood – and eating celery every day can reduce cholesterol. Being antiseptic, celery is also good for kidney problems and cystitis. Never take medicinally when pregnant.

A DISTANT RELATIVE OF wild celery, an ancient European plant, herb celery finds its natural home in marshland. Unlike the stalk celery we're more used to seeing, herb celery is a cinch to grow – and hardy to boot. It is rich in the flavonoid antioxidants vitamin A and vitamin K, plus potassium and calcium.

Herb celery is a great plant to keep in a pot near the kitchen. That way, it is easy to get to for stocks, soups, marinades, coleslaws and casseroles. All those recipes that require a stalk or two of celery for flavouring generally work perfectly well with a few leaves of herb celery instead. It also makes a wonderful accompaniment for blue cheese and cured meats.

If you grow your own leaf celery, you will find that the overwintered plants run to seed by spring. Once the seed is set, cover the plant with a bag, cut off the stem and shake to harvest the seed. Try the seeds in potato salad, cabbage dishes and breads for their hints of nutmeg and citrus, or grind them with sea salt to make celery salt with an incomparable flavour. It is perfect added to a Bloody Mary.

Horseradish

——————

This innocuous-looking parsnip imitator is, of course, a fiery, eye-watering root of the Devil. And, contrary to its name, it's no radish.

GROW
Horseradish is easy to grow, and will take over your garden if you're not careful. It prefers light, well-dug, moist soil.

EAT WITH
Beetroot, apples, tomatoes, potatoes, cabbage, chives, beef, ham, smoked fish, shellfish, walnuts, eggs, cream.

TRY
Add a dollop of grated horseradish to the meat when making burgers. Make a sauce to serve with smoked fish or fishcakes by mixing grated horseradish with crème fraîche, chives and a little lemon juice.

HEAL
Horseradish is a powerful circulatory stimulant with antibiotic properties. It has been used to help with coughs and sinus congestion and, grated into a poultice, applied externally to chilblains and stiff muscles.

A PERENNIAL NATIVE OF eastern Europe and western Asia, pungent, mustard-like horseradish is used as both a medicinal and a culinary herbaceous root. It was probably first used for culinary purposes in Russia, before spreading to eastern Europe and North America. It is a staple of Jewish Ashkenazi cuisine, notably in *chrain* – a relish that is served with gefilte fish or boiled beef and grated beetroot. In Britain, of course, it is the traditional accompaniment to roast beef.

Although it is not a radish, horseradish is in the same crucifer family, cousin to turnips, cabbages and – not surprisingly – mustard. Unpeeled, it lacks any smell to warn you what lies within. When you peel and grate it, the pungent oils in a sulphur-containing substance called sinigrin are activated (there will be tears). Making creamed horseradish sauce is a cook's rite of passage. An early English name for horseradish was red cole, which – although not referring to the root itself, which is yellowish-brown – hints at the red-hot-coals nature of its taste.

Fresh horseradish – full of calcium, sodium, magnesium and vitamin C – is at the peak of its pungency when the roots are pulled in autumn. Cooking destroys its heat, so it is usually served raw; if it is only gently warmed, its fieriness can be toned down with something soothing such as apple or cream.

Artemisia absinthium

Wormwood

*A herb with a dark reputation, wormwood is a key ingredient
in the spirit absinthe.*

GROW
If you cannot find it in the
wild and are intrigued, grow
wormwood from seed under
protection, using bark-filled
compost (soil mix). Plant
when the seedlings are large
enough to handle. Do not
grow it in gardens frequented
by children or pets.

ABSINTHE – NICKNAMED the green fairy – was the vice of
late-nineteenth-century writers and artists. In his novel *L'Assommoir*
(1877), Émile Zola wrote about the hoarse 'absinthe voice', glazed
eye and 'clammy' hand accrued by the frequent drinker. It was the
chosen poison (it's 80 per cent alcohol) of Van Gogh, Baudelaire
and Rimbaud, and, after one particularly green-fairy-filled night,
Toulouse-Lautrec was caught shooting spiders because he believed
they were about to attack him.

With feathery silver-grey leaves, stems with small, silky white
hairs and small yellow globular flower heads, wormwood can be
found growing wild on wasteland in Europe, Africa and North
America. Essentially bitter tasting, it contains thujone, a poisonous
chemical, which – although probably safe when taken in spirits such
as absinthe and vermouth – could be unsafe when taken by mouth,
causing seizures, vomiting and even paralysis.

It's no wonder, then, that legend has wormwood springing up
in the impression left in the grass by the serpent departing Eden. It
has been hung outside front doors to keep evil spirits away, and even
added to ink to stop mice from eating old letters. True to its name,
wormwood has been used to expel roundworms and threadworms
(warning: habitual use can cause convulsions); and to this day
the herb is mixed with dried lavender and mint to make a moth
repellent.

Tarragon

If the poet Ogden Nash is to be believed, 'Henry VIII divorced Catherine of Aragon because of her reckless use of tarragon.'

GROW
Sow in well-drained, slightly alkaline soil, in full sun. Pick the leaves before the plant flowers.

EAT WITH
Eggs, chicken, beef, veal, pork, fish, seafood, potatoes, tomatoes, beetroot, artichokes, asparagus, carrots, mustard, cream, goat's cheese, plums, pears, peaches, raspberries.

TRY
For tarragon vinegar, put a couple of handfuls of chopped tarragon into a jar and pour in white wine vinegar to cover. Seal and leave in a cool place for two or three weeks, shaking the jar occasionally. Strain, then pour into a sterilized bottle, adding a couple of fresh sprigs of tarragon. Seal tightly.

HEAL
Tarragon is a good source of iron, which helps the body to make red blood cells, in turn helping oxygen to move through the circulatory system. Calcium and vitamin A – good for bones and eyes – are also present.

IT'S TRUE THAT tarragon was a key constituent of the Tudor herb garden, albeit with the slightly more poetic name of dragon's wort. So much is indicated by the herb's Latin name: *dracunculus* is a French corruption of the Latin for 'dragon', and tarragon was said to soothe snakebites. The modern French for tarragon, *l'estragon*, means 'little dragon'.

It does not have a fiery taste, of course: the flavour is warming and refined, with subtle liquorice tones. This herb has always been central to French cuisine: most cooks have *poulet à l'estragon* as part of their repertoire, and it is a leading figure in *fines herbes*, made with co-stars parsley, chervil and chives and used in meat, fish and egg dishes. Béarnaise sauce, the classic accompaniment to steak, would be nothing without the aniseedy notes of tarragon to provide a counterpoint to all that richness. Tarragon vinegar is indispensable for giving a lift to sauces and salad dressings. Like many of the anise-flavoured herbs, tarragon makes an unexpected yet pleasing partner for fruit: try it with peaches, plums, raspberries or pears, but be careful not to overdo it.

With the Persian saying 'Even the worm inside a stone eats herbs' in mind, the food writer and cultural anthropologist Claudia Roden explains the ancient Persian custom for women of eating a bowl of fresh herbs with bread and cheese at the end of a meal: 'According to an old belief, this will help them to keep their husbands away from a rival.' Tarragon was in the mix – along with chives (page 23), mint (page 119) and dill (page 31). Any herbs work, in fact, nicely arranged in a bowl.

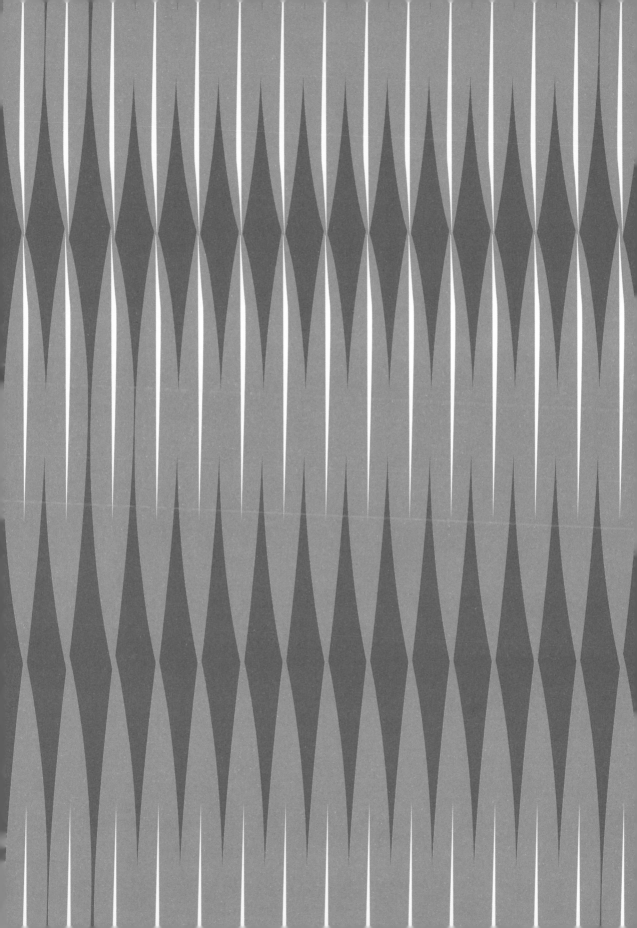

Artemisia vulgaris

Mugwort

Sounding like something the fictional teenage wizard Harry Potter might eat, mugwort is the first herb mentioned in the tenth-century Anglo-Saxon song 'The Nine Herbs Charm'.

GROW

Grow mugwort in full sun and rich, moist soil, harvesting it before it flowers. Be careful: It can get out of control.

EAT WITH

Beans, game, duck, goose, oily fish, pork, onions, rice, potatoes, noodles.

TRY

Add a few sprigs of mugwort to an apple stuffing or apple sauce for goose or duck. Substitute mugwort for watercress in potato and watercress soup.

HEAL

Mugwort is used in moxibustion, a treatment similar to acupuncture, in which dried mugwort is ground and formed into a cigar-shaped stick, then burned on patients' skin to strengthen the immune system, blood and life energy. Mugwort tea cleanses the liver and promotes good sleep.

'THE NINE HERBS CHARM' forms part of the *Lacnunga*, or *Remedies*, an Anglo-Saxon herbal. The Anglo-Saxons needed a lot of remedies: they believed diseases were spread by toxins blowing in the wind. Songs, salt, water and herbs were all used as cures. Practitioners were encouraged to sing 'The Nine Herbs Charm' three times – into the mouth of the wounded, into their ears and over the wound – before applying the salve, the recipe for which was held in the song. 'Remember, mugwort,' the charm goes, 'you have the power against poison and against infection, you have the power against the loathsome foe roving through the land.' These days, mugwort has been used to assist digestion and liver function and to relax the nervous system – although it should not be taken during pregnancy.

A herbaceous perennial that grows wild throughout North and South America, Europe and Asia, mugwort has an aroma of juniper and pepper, with a light hint of sweet mint and a mildly bitter aftertaste. It works well with oily fish and fatty meat, such as duck or goose, since it aids digestion. In Japan, it is often paired with rice cakes and soba noodles; in Korea, *ssukguk* is a traditional soup made of mugwort and clams; in Germany, it is a popular herb called *Gänsekraut*, or 'goose herb', often added to gravies.

Orach

———

Coming from the Latin aurago, *meaning 'golden', and cultivated in both Europe and temperate Asia, spinach-like orach belongs to the goosefoot family.*

GROW
Sow orach seeds two or three weeks before the last frost is expected. Orach can grow to a spindly 2 m (6 ft) high, but it should remain bushy if you harvest the leaves regularly. It likes heat and some sun.

EAT WITH
Spinach, sorrel and other salad greens, fennel, potatoes, lamb, game, fish.

TRY
Add young red orach leaves to salads for an instant splash of colour. Cook orach briefly in olive oil with a little crushed garlic until wilted, then serve with grilled fish or lamb. Add wilted red orach to a risotto or pilaff for pink-tinged rice.

HEAL
Like other green leaves, orach stimulates digestion, reducing the chance of constipation. It also has slightly laxative and diuretic effects, thus stimulating urination, which helps to purify the kidneys. The high level of vitamin C is a great boost for the immune system.

ITS OLDER POPULAR name is mountain spinach, and one online purveyor today advertises it as 'mountain spinach for merry pranksters' – although it is not related to Popeye's favourite vegetable. In fact, orach was popular in sixteenth-century England, where, according to the herbalist William Salmon, it grew 'by Walls, old Hedges, Ditch sides and Dunghills'. It eventually lost out to spinach, however, which seemingly became easier to grow, and has a more succulent leaf.

Wild orach can be quite bitter, although the cultivated kind has a rather meaty flavour, with a suggestion of fennel. Like spinach, it releases plenty of liquid during cooking. There are several varieties of orach, with handsome red, white or green arrow-headed leaves. Green orach can have red-tinged stems, while red orach has deep, plummy leaves and stems. Like spinach, orach contains some fantastic nutrients, including vitamin C (twice the amount that lemon has), vitamin K and plenty of calcium, carotenes and iron. A word of caution, though: like spinach, it contains significant amounts of oxalic acid, which forms the insoluble salts found in kidney stones.

Daisy

‘*Daisy, daisy, give me your answer, do. I’m half crazy,
all for the love of you.*’

HARRY DACRE, ‘DAISY BELL’, 1892

GROW
If daisies don’t already grow
in your garden, you can
buy the seeds from online
stockists. Grow in rich, moist,
well-drained soil in full sun.

EAT WITH
Green salads, fruit salads,
as a garnish for cakes and
mousses.

TRY
Deep-fry daisies in a light
tempura batter, drain on
paper towels and serve
sprinkled with sugar. Make
daisy tea by adding daisies to
freshly boiled water, infusing
for five to ten minutes, then
straining for a subtle, lemony
taste.

HEAL
Daisy can be used topically
on small wounds, sores and
scratches. A tincture can be
used as a mouthwash for
sore throats, and chewing
the leaves can relieve
mouth ulcers.

USED BY THE HERBALIST John Gerard as a cure for wounds and liver disorders, the common daisy is a much-loved herb plant. Also called herb Margaret, bruisewort and goose flower, the daisy forms a rosette of spoon-shaped leaves with classic flower heads that can only be described as daisy-like. Famously, daisies are used by children in the game of love and life – ‘She loves me, she loves me not’ – where they gradually pick off all the petals to divine the love of the other. Rather enjoyably, the Russian lines for this famous game are more full-on: ‘She loves me, she loves me not; she kisses me, she kisses me not; she presses me to her heart, she presses me not; she curses me to the Devil, she curses me not.’

Besides being used in an insect-repellent spray made from an infusion of the leaves, daisies have long been thought to help heal wounds. A recent study seems to confirm this. They have also been used to relieve coughs, colds and catarrh. Indeed, a modern analysis of daisies shows that they contain more vitamin C than lemons.

Young daisy leaf shoots are delicious eaten raw or cooked. Add the buds and flowers to salads – their bitter-honey quality is a perfect match for lettuce. They are beautiful, of course, added to fruit salads and used as decorations for cakes.

Borage

So the old adage goes: borage for courage.

GROW
Borage needs a dedicated space in which to grow. Sow seed in well-drained soil after the last frost. Allow the plant to go to seed, thinning out unwanted seedlings, since it is an enthusiastic self-seeder.

EAT WITH
Fish, eel, potatoes, peas, cucumber, white cheese, fruit.

TRY
Scatter the flowers over salads. Stir shredded young leaves (older ones are too prickly) into a summery pea soup. Cook peeled, deseeded half-moons of cucumber gently in butter for about five minutes, then stir in finely shredded young borage leaves, a squeeze of lemon and some salt.

HEAL
The dried leaves can be brewed into a tea, which is said to reduce a high temperature (borage's Arabic name means 'the father of the sweat'). Borage can be taken as a supplement or in liquid extract form for its essential fatty acids and high levels of calcium and iron.

ESSENTIALLY A SALAD herb, borage was said by early herbalists to foster cheerfulness and courage. The seventeenth-century scholar Robert Burton included borage beneath the engraved frontispiece of his classic book *The Anatomy of Melancholy* (1621), 'to cheer the heart of those black fumes which make it smart'.

You can tell this herb was of interest to medicinal herbalists: the clue is in the Latin word *officinalis*, meaning 'used in medicine' – from the noun *officina*, which originally meant 'workshop', then 'monastic storeroom' and finally 'pharmacy'. And a pharmacist's herb this is indeed: it was used to treat lung disease, hence its other name, lungwort (*wort* being Anglo-Saxon for 'medicinal herb'). Borage leaves and flowers are rich in potassium and calcium, which can purify the blood.

Borage has rough, hairy leaves and blue (occasionally white and pink) flowers, beloved of bees. Its year-round colourfulness means that gardeners love borage too, although it tends to spread easily, so they do have to keep it in line.

Borage flowers can often be seen garnishing a Pimm's cocktail in the summer. The gentle cucumber flavour of both flowers and leaves makes them good to combine with cucumber in salads. In parts of the Mediterranean, the leaves are cooked and eaten as a vegetable.

Calamint

―――――――

Thriving in sandy soil, calamint releases a strong camphor scent when the leaves are crushed.

GROW
Calamint makes an excellent border plant, but take care to keep it from invading other areas. It grows neatly in a container of well-drained soil, particularly if placed in full sun.

EAT WITH
Artichokes, green beans, mushrooms, potatoes, chicken, lamb, beef, rabbit, fish, seafood, lemon.

TRY
Add calamint to sautéed mushrooms, with a little chilli, if you like. Scatter it over pasta dishes or risottos or add to stuffings for vegetables.

HEAL
Calamint has long been used as a medicinal herb, its high menthol content making it useful as a poultice for bruises and contusions.

THE NAME CALAMINT is said to come from the Greek *kalos*, meaning 'good' or 'noble', because of the ancient belief that the herb could save you from the stunning gaze of the basilisk, the fabled king of the serpents.

Calamint is a thick-stemmed, bushy herb with heavily veined leaves and furry, fuzzy foliage. *Calamintha nepeta* is in fact known as lesser calamint and deemed to have superior qualities among the *Calamintha* varieties. It forms a compact mound of shiny, green, strongly toothed, oregano-like leaves, with lavender-pink flowers and a scent that is a cross between mint and marjoram; it will be your nose that finds it first. It grows wildly and profusely, needing little by way of water.

Known as *nepitella* or *mentuccia* in Italy, calamint is a staple of Tuscan cooking. In Rome, it is mixed with breadcrumbs, garlic, parsley and olive oil as a stuffing for artichokes, and is also added to tripe.

Calendula officinalis and *Tagetes* species

Marigold

Open afresh your round of starry folds,
Ye ardent marigolds!

JOHN KEATS, 'I STOOD TIP-TOE UPON A LITTLE HILL', 1816

GROW
Marigolds thrive in moderately fertile, well-drained soil. Sow directly in the garden once the soil is warm, or start indoors six weeks before the last frost is expected. They also do well in pots.

EAT WITH
Rice, eggs, salad leaves, peppers, beetroot, cream, fish, chicken, soft cheese.

TRY
For a bright colour and delicate flavour, add marigold petals to rice or egg dishes as they cook. Infuse milk with marigold petals to give it a golden hue – it can then be used in cooking. Strew the petals over a green salad or over beetroot or red peppers for a vibrant effect.

HEAL
Marigold has been used medicinally since the days of ancient Egypt. It can be used as an antiseptic eyewash, as well as a tincture for bee stings and warts. It can be also taken as a tea, in a sitz bath (an old-fashioned aroma-filled bath to soothe the perineum) or added to juice.

THIS SHORT-LIVED MARIGOLD *Calendula*, native to southern Europe, was once simply called 'golds'. Garlands of them were worn as an emblem of jealousy by hard-done-by lovers. *Calendula* is so-called because of the plant's reputation for blooming on the calends (the first day of each month throughout the year). The shorter *Tagetes*, which is native to Africa and to North and South America and bears flowers in varying mixtures of orange, yellow and dark red, is used in Mexico to decorate graves for the Day of the Dead. With its bright yellow and orange inflorescences (groups of flowers arranged on a main stem), *Calendula* is a strikingly cheerful plant that will easily attract butterflies to any herb garden.

The flowers are not just attractive but also useful. The practice of cooking with flowers dates back to the time of the ancient Greeks, who pioneered herbal remedies with lavender flowers, and to the Romans, who flavoured wine with roses and violets. In England, marigold flowers were once used to colour cheese, and as a substitute for saffron – although there is no comparison in terms of flavour. There is a recipe for marigold wine in *The Receipt Book of Charles Carter* (1732), which advises putting 'in your marigold flowers a little bruised but not much stamp'd, a Peck to each gallon'. Nowadays, marigolds – with their varyingly spicy, bitter and tangy flavours – might be added to butters, fish soups, salads, cookies, custards and cakes.

Carline

———

*In the Middle Ages, an angel was supposed to have shown the
French ruler Charlemagne how to use carline thistle against
the plague epidemic that was killing his soldiers.*

GROW
It is easy to grow carline:
sow seed in a cold frame
in spring, then plant out
the seedlings in summer.
They like plenty of sun.

HEAL
The essential oils of the
carline root have been
shown to have some antiviral
properties, and are used in
supplements to treat colds
and flu.

THE HERB WAS named, therefore, after Charlemagne, whose
name means 'Charles the Great'. In medieval times this thistle
was said to help anyone carrying it to gather strength from other
people, and even from animals. Another belief was that the thistle
root could give a man the sexual strength and potency of a stallion;
for this to happen, it had to be planted and harvested under a new
moon at the stroke of midnight and fertilized with the sperm of
a black stallion. Carline thistle is still carried in some parts of the
world today as protection against harm. It is also used as a natural
barometer (the French name for it is *baromètre*): the flower closes
when the air becomes humid, usually an indicator of bad weather.

The carline is a stemless European perennial with sharp,
dandelion-like leaves arranged radially in a circle on the ground.
It is generally found on slopes, wasteland and pastures, and prefers
limestone soil. Since its beautiful flowers can be eaten in a similar
way to globe artichokes, carline is sometimes called hunter's bread.
The root can be harvested in autumn and dried for use in tea.

Camomile

Like a camomile bed –
The more it is trodden
The more it will spread.

TRADITIONAL RHYME

GROW
Start from seed indoors about six weeks before the last frost is expected. Plant the seedlings in the sunnier parts of your garden, or in containers. Camomile seeds itself readily; let some of the blossoms go to seed rather than picking them all.

EAT WITH
Apricots, peaches, strawberries, apples, vanilla, lamb, fish, honey, lemon.

TRY
Infuse the cream for pannacotta with fresh camomile flowers for a delicate scent and flavour, then serve the set pannacotta with strawberries. Scatter fresh camomile flowers over a simple iced cake that has had a couple of tablespoons of dried camomile added to the batter.

HEAL
In Beatrix Potter's story, Peter Rabbit's mother famously 'put him to bed, and made some camomile tea' for him. It can help with insomnia, aid digestion and – as a cool compress – relieve tired eyes.

EVOCATIVE OF SUMMERS filled with dappled light, camomile lawns were made famous by Mary Wesley, whose novel *The Camomile Lawn* (1984) was set in Cornwall. The apple-like scent associated with camomile (its Greek name means earth-apple) is partly responsible for the horticultural habit of growing camomile lawns – although there is also a certain amount of justified laziness involved, since a camomile lawn requires much less maintenance than grass and releases a pleasant scent underfoot. Creeping thymes such as *Thymus serpyllum* go well with camomile in a herb lawn, but you cannot just add them to existing grass, as the grass will compete (and win); the whole lawn must be sown from herbs.

Native to Europe, camomile is an age-old medicinal herb, known in ancient Egypt, Greece and Rome. It was seen as the answer to many of life's ailments, including asthma, colic, fever, nausea and skin diseases – very much the European version of the Chinese wonder herb ginseng (page 147). There are many different cultivars of camomile – all daisy-like plants of the Asteraceae family – and each requires its own set of conditions to grow. German camomile has a sweeter flavour when drunk as a tea, whereas Roman camomile has a bitterer taste. The herbalist John Gerard said the stinking camomile variety had a 'naughty smell'.

Fat Hen

———

*Also known as lamb's quarters, white goose, dirty dick, pigweed
and muckweed, fat hen is the great secret of the herb world.*

GROW
Sow fat hen seeds in rich,
well-drained soil in a
sunny spot.

EAT WITH
Cheese, fish, anchovies,
cream, eggs, onions,
tomatoes, potatoes.

TRY
Substitute fat hen for
spinach in curries, gnocchi,
pasta dishes and savoury
tarts. Blend young fat hen
leaves with garlic, pine nuts,
Parmesan cheese and olive
oil to make pesto.

HEAL
In traditional Indian medicine,
powder from dried fat hen
leaves is used to treat burns.
A decoction can be made
from the stalks and leaves
and rubbed into arthritic
joints and sunburn.

IDENTIFIED IN THE stomach of the Iron Age Tollund Man,
fat hen was effectively the food supplement of primitive peoples,
although, as its name suggests, it is now mostly considered chicken
fodder. Rich in iron, calcium and vitamin C, this cousin of the
rather brilliantly named Good King Henry (sometimes used as a
cough remedy for sheep) is a quiet but potentially powerful player in
the world of herbs and deserves much greater recognition. After all,
its leaves are more nutritious than spinach and cabbage.

Since it can grow anywhere, often being found in hedges
and fields and near old walls, fat hen is easily cultivated. Its iron-
rich leaves and young shoots can be sautéed in a little butter and
seasoned with a grating of nutmeg. When young, the leaves can be
consumed raw in salads and cooked in casseroles and savoury pies.
Older leaves can be used in the same way as spinach. Like spinach,
they reduce greatly in volume when cooked, so you will need a lot
more than you think.

Cichorium intybus

Chicory

The woody herb chicory has bright blue flowers that – legend has it – are the metamorphosed eyes of a young woman, weeping for the loss of her lover's ship.

GROW
This tall herb needs well-drained soil that is deep enough to accommodate its very long taproots.

EAT WITH
Peppers, salad greens, chilli, nuts, bacon, ham, blue cheese, honey, orange.

TRY
Blanch chicory greens briefly in boiling water, then drain well and cook gently in olive oil with garlic and dried chilli. Cut radicchio heads into quarters, coat with olive oil and chargrill until wilted and tender.

HEAL
Chicory contains beneficial probiotics, good for combating indigestion and heartburn. It can help to reduce cholesterol and to ease the pain of conditions such as osteoarthritis. In a gel, it can soothe sore muscles. It is not suitable for pregnant women.

IT'S EASY TO see why this herb is associated with vulnerability and bereavement: the flowers last only a day (they're replaced the next) and close in the midday sun.

There's some confusion when it comes to the common names. Endive (*Cichorium endive*) is a related leaf from the same family as chicory (*C. intybus*); in the United States the curly form of endive is often called chicory. In Europe, chicory (*C. intybus*) is a popular salad vegetable, a variety of which is forced into tight, leafy heads called chicons, which are sometimes called Belgian endive.

Chicory leaves are used in summer salads in the Liguria and Apulia regions of Italy, as well as Catalonia, Greece and Turkey. The roots can be roasted, ground and drunk as a coffee substitute on account of their pleasing bitterness; Charles Dickens wrote about this in *Household Words*. The chicons of the cultivated Belgian *witloof* variety (*witloof* means 'white leaf') go famously with Gruyère cheese and ham. Radicchio, also known as red chicory, is the other well-known cultivated variety, which can be grilled or roasted.

Miner's Lettuce

So-called because it was eaten by the California Gold Rush miners for its scurvy-preventing vitamin C, miner's lettuce is America's gift to salad.

GROW
Sow this cool-season plant a month before the first frost is expected, repeating every two weeks until mid-spring for a continuous harvest.

EAT WITH
Rocket (arugula), sorrel, watercress, soft cheese, potatoes, eggs, fish.

TRY
Add miner's lettuce to thick yogurt with some crushed garlic, chopped mint and salt and pepper. Sprinkle with a little cayenne pepper and serve as a dip or salad.

HEAL
High in chlorophyll and vitamin C, miner's lettuce can cleanse the liver of toxins and heavy metals and give the immune system a general boost.

THIS LEAFY HERB was brought from North America to Europe by the great Scots naturalist Archibald Menzies in the late eighteenth century. In a journal entry in 1792, Menzies wrote: 'A little before the Fog dispersd. . .we walkd along the shore. . .In this walk I found growing in the Crevices of a small rock about midway between the two points a new Species of Claytonia & as I met with it no where else in my journeys, it must be considered as rare a plant in this country.'

Also known as winter purslane, claytonia and spring beauty, this rosette-forming plant can grow to as little as 1 cm (½ in.) or as tall as 40 cm (16 in.). It tends to appear on chaparral in woodlands, forests, orchards and coastal regions in North America. The best will grow under trees, preferring cool, damp conditions but often springing up in the sunshine after rainy periods. Some indigenous American tribes used to strew miner's lettuce along the pathways of a type of ant; the acid from the ants' excrement would make a kind of vinaigrette to eat with the lettuce.

Miner's lettuce has a lemony flavour, rather like that of sorrel (see page 172). It is a robust leaf that can be treated like spinach and also works well in salads. A useful source of vitamin C, it is one of the few salad leaves that will keep growing throughout the winter in temperate climates.

Convallaria majalis

Lily of the Valley

———

The sixteenth-century herbalist John Gerard recommended a rather unorthodox concoction made from lily of the valley: 'Put into a glass and set it in a hill of ants, firmly closed for one month. After which you will find a liquor that when applied appeaseth the paine and grief of gout.'

GROW
Sow seeds in pots or in the garden, in fertile soil with some leaf mould. Make sure the soil is in the shade, and water regularly.

HEAL
Use this herb only with the expert advice of a qualified practitioner; it can be poisonous if misused. Lily of the valley can, however, be used to treat heart disease, lung conditions and burns, and to relieve depression.

A NATIVE OF EUROPE and North America, deadly lily of the valley was made famous by the television show *Breaking Bad*, when the chemistry teacher protagonist Walt poisoned six-year-old Brock with its red berries to topple the drug kingpin Gustavo Fring. It is a beautiful plant, with bell-like flowers, and prefers growing in shady woodland to the open valley of its name. It flourishes in deeply cultivated, well-rotted manure or leaf mould.

Lily of the valley is associated with some significant weepers: it is alleged to have been born from the tears of the Virgin Mary, shed at the foot of the Cross; from the tears of Mary Magdalene when she found Christ's tomb; and from the tears of Eve, found crying after she and Adam were expelled from the Garden of Eden. The flower also has associations with chastity and purity, and is often included in bridal arrangements. Medieval monks saw lily of the valley as a ladder to heaven, naming it as such, because of the heavenly stairway made by the lovely white flowers.

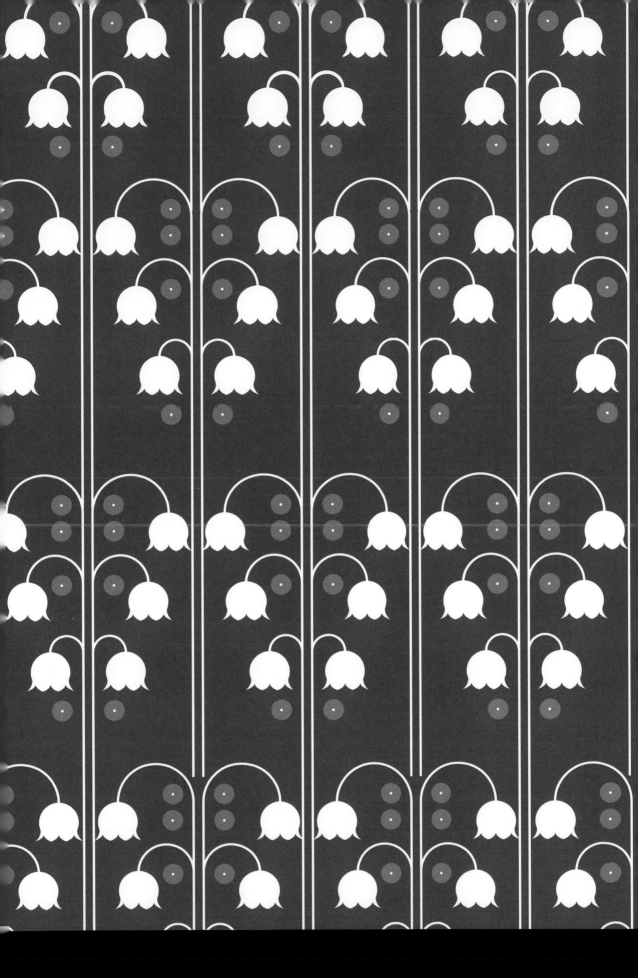

Coriander

———

Coriander, or cilantro as it is often called in the United States, is very much a love-it-or-hate-it herb.

TO SOME, IT is beautifully delicate, with a lemon-ginger aroma and hints of pepper, lemon, orange and sage to the taste; to others, it is as disagreeable as chewing on a floral soap. A staple of Asian, Latin American and Portuguese cuisines, coriander should be used generously for the most impact.

Coriander has been cultivated for more than 3,000 years and used not just in cooking but also as part of the herbalist's medicine cabinet – in particular to treat dyspepsia, flatulence and loss of appetite. All parts of the plant can be eaten: as well as the fragrant leaves, the seeds are an aromatic spice, the stalks are added to spice pastes and the roots are used in Thai and Indian dishes. The leaves are best added towards the end of cooking, since prolonged heat reduces the intensity of the flavour. Try coriander in everything from stir-fries and curries to chutneys, relishes and salads. It makes a piquant dressing with chillies, garlic and lime juice. Indeed, coriander is the base herb for some brilliantly named dishes: zhug, chermoula, ceviche and guacamole.

Mitsuba

Also known as Japanese wild parsley, mitsuba covers Japan's mountains with beautiful star-shaped, pale-purple blossoms and looks like the love child of parsley and perilla.

GROW

Sow from seed in rich soil, repeating every six weeks for a continuous supply. Keep the soil moist and you'll be harvesting continuously between spring and autumn. Mitsuba can grow quite tall (up to 1 m/3 ft), and seeds itself readily.

EAT WITH

Eggs, fish, seafood, chicken, noodles, rice, carrots, mushrooms.

TRY

Substitute mitsuba for parsley in salads and as a garnish for vegetable dishes. Dust mitsuba leaves with a little flour, dip in tempura batter and deep-fry.

HEAL

Mitsuba is used to treat the common cold, fever and haemorrhages. It can also help to relieve stress.

MEANING 'THREE LEAVES' — not surprisingly, three leaves grow on each of the tall, skinny stems — mitsuba is an attractive pale-green herb that flourishes in the shade (although it doesn't mind a bit of sun). The serrated trefoil leaves are large and tender, with a subtle flavour that is a cross between parsley, celery and chervil.

Mitsuba has been used medicinally for various purposes, but is more familiar now as a culinary ingredient, making a star appearance in the Japanese seafood soup *matsutake dobinmushi*. Enjoyed during the brief period (in September and November) when the wonderfully fragrant pine mushrooms are available, this is a delicate broth made in a teapot with thin slices of chicken, shrimp, ginkgo nuts (see page 96) and mitsuba. More regularly, mitsuba is used in stir-fries, sukiyaki, sashimi, custards and rice, and as a garnish for miso soup and *nabe*, a variety of communal one-pot meal. It can turn bitter when cooked for more than a few minutes, so always add it towards the end of cooking.

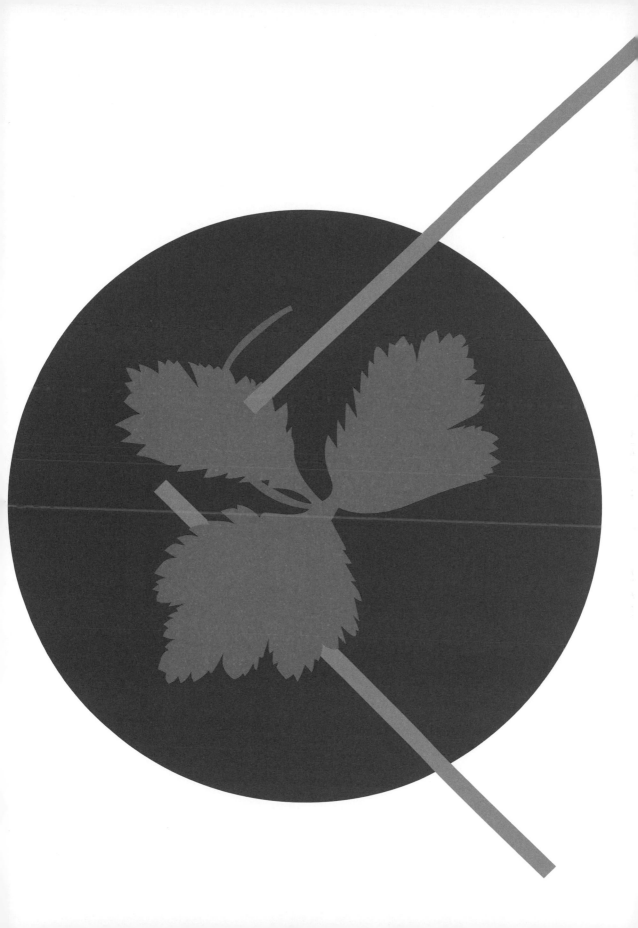

Cymbopogon citratus

Lemongrass

*A perennial grass of tropical Asia and other warm climates,
lemongrass grows with abundance in the right conditions.*

GROW
Lemongrass makes an excellent container plant. Sow the seeds in trays under protection at 20°C (70°F); it will grow successfully only when the night temperature does not fall below 8°C (47°F).

EAT WITH
Fish, seafood, meat, noodles, rice, mango, lime, papaya, ginger, garlic, basil, mint, star anise, chilli, tamarind, coconut.

TRY
Make a syrup by gently heating together 200 g (7 oz) sugar and 300 ml (10 fl. oz) water, adding six crushed and sliced lemongrass stalks and 30 g (1 oz) finely chopped fresh ginger. Simmer for five minutes, then leave to cool. Strain and chill. Pour the syrup over exotic fruit salads, or add sparkling water for a refreshing drink.

HEAL
Being rich in iron, zinc, magnesium and vitamins A, B and C, lemongrass can help the body to maintain healthy cholesterol levels, reduce fever and strengthen the immune system. Lemongrass tea can improve the quality of sleep.

ALSO KNOWN AS fever grass, citronella and takrai, lemongrass – true to its name – releases a lemony flavour when crushed. It is a key herb in Thai cooking, but is also used in Thailand as everything from a snake repellent and a preserving agent for ancient manuscripts to a pesticide and a key element of Ayurvedic medicine.

To prepare lemongrass for cooking, peel off the tough outer layers, bash the stem to crush it lightly, and chop it finely. Besides Thailand, it is also used in India, Vietnam, Indonesia and Malaysia, adding a cooling contrast to the chilli heat of curries, laksas, soups, stir-fries, spice pastes and marinades. Its citrus flavour works equally well in desserts, including sorbets and creams. Smashed lemongrass stems can be made into a tea, served hot or chilled. Good for relaxing the stomach, this herb is wonderful paired with ginger.

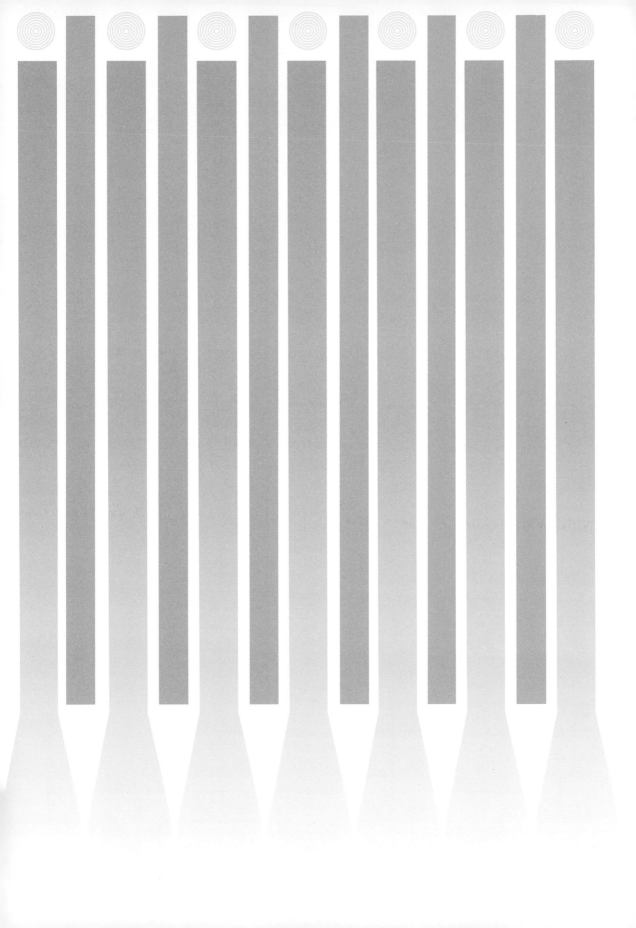

Cardoon

―――――――

One of the most impressively structural herbs, with
flamboyant, spiky purple flower buds, cardoon is a thistle-like
native of the Mediterranean and North Africa.

GROW
Find a sheltered, wind-free
spot and sow seeds in fertile,
well-drained soil.

EAT WITH
Anchovies, cheese, seafood,
pork, ham, poultry, potatoes,
mushrooms, onions, beans.

TRY
Make a *bagna cauda* by
gently heating two crushed
garlic cloves and half a
can of anchovy fillets in
2 tablespoons of olive oil,
stirring until the anchovies
dissolve. Gradually stir in
90 ml (3 fl. oz) olive oil and
25 g (1 oz) butter and warm
through. Bring the pan to
the table and dip blanched
cardoon stalks into the sauce
while it is still warm.

HEAL
Containing phytonutrients,
B-complex vitamins and
vitamin C, as well as vital
minerals such as calcium and
iron, cardoon can promote a
healthy liver and lower blood
cholesterol.

INTRODUCED TO URUGUAY, they must have been quite a sight
for Charles Darwin, who in 1831 came across a whole field of this
distinctive weed-turned-herb, growing in thickets and reaching the
height of horses, in the settlement of Guardia del Monte.

The cardoon – *cardo* in Latin means 'thistle' – has thick, celery-
like stalks, feathery, silvery foliage and, being a relative of the globe
artichoke (*Cynara scolymus*), a distinctive and delicate taste. Very
popular in Victorian Britain, it subsequently fell out of favour until
enterprising chefs recently started adding it to their menus. Cardoon
is time-consuming to prepare: the stalks need substantial trimming
before the celery-like strings are peeled, dunked in acidulated water
to prevent browning, and blanched to tame the bitterness. This effort
is rewarded with a juicy texture and a fine flavour reminiscent of
artichokes.

This plant has always been appreciated in continental Europe,
growing wild and in market gardens in France, Italy and Spain.
The stalks are sometimes eaten raw in Italy, dipped into *bagna cauda*,
a warm anchovy sauce. The flower buds can be treated in the same
way as young artichokes, while the leaves are cooked in broths, braises
and gratins. In Spain they feature in a Christmas special, the *cocido
madrileño*, a slow-cooked meat and vegetable dish along the lines of the
French *pot-au-feu*. In Portugal and France the dried flowers have been
used in the past as a substitute for rennet in cheese-making.

Dysphania ambrosioides

Epazote

Also known as wormseed and Mexican tea, epazote is earthy, minty and camphorous, with a pungent, bitter taste and citrus notes.

GROW
You just need a lot of sun, that's all. Epazote is an annual, but will seed itself. Once it is established, overwinter the plants indoors.

EAT WITH
Sweetcorn, mushrooms, onions, squash, peppers, green vegetables, fish, shellfish, chorizo, pork, rice, lime, coriander, garlic, oregano, eggs, white cheese.

TRY
Add a few epazote leaves to a black bean chilli or to bean soups. Stir chopped epazote into omelettes or scrambled eggs, along with some cumin seeds and a little finely chopped fresh chilli.

HEAL
Epazote leaves in cooking counter indigestion and flatulence, providing large amounts of dietary fibre and protein. Native Mayans drank infusions of the herb to prevent worm infestation, thanks to its high ascaridole levels.

THE ODD SMELL – kerosene-like to some, lemony to others – is in the name: a member of the goosefoot family, epazote derives its name from the Aztec Nahuatl word for 'skunk sweat'. Native to central and southern Mexico, epazote was essential to Mayan cuisine in the Yucatán and Guatemala. It is now an important ingredient in the cooking of Mexico and the Caribbean – and, to an extent, North America, where it can be found as a roadside weed. It is often paired with coriander and cumin.

Prolific once sown – no surprise there, given that it is a Mexican relative of fat hen (see page 60) – epazote is most often used in bean dishes (helpfully, it can reduce flatulence). It can be added raw to salsas, but it is better cooked – thrown into dishes during the last fifteen minutes of cooking to prevent bitterness. Epazote is an essential component of *mole verde* and quesadillas: just one leaf per quesadilla should be enough. It is said to aid digestion and cut through all that cheese. If you grow your own, it is possible, come autumn, to dry the leaves, flowers and seeds for use in the winter.

Echinacea

From echinos, *the Greek word for 'hedgehog', because of the prickly scales in its large, conical seed head, this is one outstanding and contentious herb.*

GROW
An attractive garden plant in its own right, echinacea needs full sun and fertile, well-drained soil. Avoid damp spots. Sow seeds under cover as early as possible in the year to allow for maximum growth.

TRY
Dry the cone part of the flower and use in floral arrangements. Make an echinacea tea with dried echinacea leaves, lemongrass (page 72), spearmint (page 122) and stevia leaves (page 188) to taste.

HEAL
It is said that Native Americans watched wounded elk seek and eat echinacea for their afflictions – they called it elk root – which taught them to use the herb likewise. Echinacea can be taken as an infusion of fresh leaves for colds, chills and the flu. Tinctures can be used for urinary infections; mouthwash for sore throats; and an echinacea cream rubbed into boils and sores. Caution: high doses can cause nausea.

WITH TALL STEMS that bear single pink or purple flowers, and a central purple or brown cone-shaped seed head, echinacea – essentially a giant purple daisy – is arguably the paracetamol of the herb world.

Archaeologists have found evidence that Native Americans used echinacea more than 400 years ago to treat infections and wounds, and as a general cure-all. Indeed, echinacea has been used throughout history to cure everything from venomous snake and insect bites and scarlet fever to syphilis and blood poisoning. The Eclectics, a group of American herbalists practising from the 1850s to the 1930s, observed its effects in hospitals, claiming it could treat gangrene, bronchitis, typhoid and smallpox, among other deadly diseases. Even they couldn't agree about it, however, and Harvey Wickes Felter, one of the Eclectic physicians, admitted that there was 'no satisfactory explanation' of how echinacea worked.

It's a strongly debated topic. There have been over 350 scientific research studies into the herb, discovering that it contains all kinds of therapeutic elements: polysaccharides, glycoproteins, alkamides and flavonoids. Some studies have demonstrated that echinacea increases the activity of white blood cells, others that it boosts interferon production (interferon attacks viruses). However, many peer-reviewed journal articles have been criticized for selective reporting. Despite the controversy about its efficacy, plenty of people reach for echinacea to shorten the duration of common colds and sore throats and boost the immune system. Of course, this must be done only in consultation with a doctor.

Elsholtzia ciliata

Vietnamese Balm

———

Reportedly spotted growing in America in the late nineteenth century, Vietnamese balm is more commonly found in eastern and central Asia. It has saw-edged leaves and flowers that bloom in flat purple spikes.

GROW
This European perennial (an annual in the U.S.) can be grown outdoors from seed after the last frost. If using cuttings, encourage them to root by standing them in water; once rooted, transplant into light, moist soil, keeping the plant out of the shade.

EAT WITH
Cucumber, lettuce, mushrooms, chicken, fish, seafood, rice, noodles, galangal, chilli, coriander, garlic, mint.

TRY
Put together a platter of fresh herbs, with plenty of Vietnamese balm, and serve as a cooling accompaniment to Vietnamese or Thai dishes.

HEAL
Vietnamese balm is used to prevent flatulence and relieve the effects of excessive alcohol, and – when added to steam baths – can improve skin. The Vietnamese make a tea from it to soothe stomach complaints.

WITH A CLEAN, LEMONY SCENT (and perhaps even a suggestion of mint), the flavour is something between lemon balm and lemongrass; indeed, those two can be used in lieu of Vietnamese balm. It is used in egg and fish dishes, grilled meats, soups, noodles and rice. The zesty flavour brightens up pretty much any dish – try it in Vietnamese summer rolls. If you cannot find Vietnamese balm in the shops – and you would need to search out an oriental supermarket – it is worth trying to grow it yourself. You can harvest the leaves from spring until August.

Rocket

—————

*This peppery salad herb – called arugula in the United States –
is given its pungent kick by compounds called aldehydes. It has
been eaten since Roman times but was then almost forgotten
and has only recently come back into favour.*

GROW
Rocket is easy to grow from
seed. You can get a crop
throughout the year if you
make frequent small sowings
(don't sow too thickly). It loves
a bit of shade and should be
ready to pick within six to
eight weeks.

EAT WITH
Fish, seafood, Parma ham,
chicken, beef, lamb, goat's
cheese, Parmesan cheese, soft
cheese, tomatoes, avocado,
peppers, potatoes, chilli,
anchovies, pasta, rice, polenta.

TRY
Make a crab and rocket
sandwich: mix fresh crab
meat with mayonnaise, lemon
juice, finely chopped chilli and
parsley. Sandwich in buttered
crusty bread or brown bread
with a generous helping of
young rocket leaves.

HEAL
Rocket can decrease the
risk of obesity, heart disease
and diabetes, and promote a
healthy complexion, increased
energy and overall lower
weight. Reach for rocket
before a run – the high nitrate
levels can be beneficial while
exercising.

BEFORE IT WAS a fashionable side salad, rocket was 'applied to
Wounds made by the bitings of Mad Dogs, or of Serpents, as the
Viper, Rattle-snake' (William Salmon). Once their culinary charms
were discovered, the toothed leaves remained popular well into the
eighteenth century in Europe. It remains a mystery why they then
fell out of favour for two centuries everywhere except in Italy. The
recent rocket revival in Europe and North America can only be a
good thing. This delicious, peppery leaf has become ubiquitous.

Rocket is stuffed with phytochemicals, antioxidants, vitamins
and minerals. Its warm pepperiness has made it the go-to herb for
everything from heaped salads to pizzas (add a shower of rocket
just before serving), from sandwiches to pesto, and from grills and
roasts to pasta and rice dishes. Its punchy character has helped it to
become the salad leaf for people who don't like salad. Sometimes,
though, less is more, and rocket tends to work better in combination
with other leaves to offset its pushy flavour. Young leaves are
relatively mild and sweet; older ones are more assertive but lose
their bite when cooked, for example in a soup or a pasta sauce.
Add the flowers to dishes for a piquant flavour and to stand out
from the crowd.

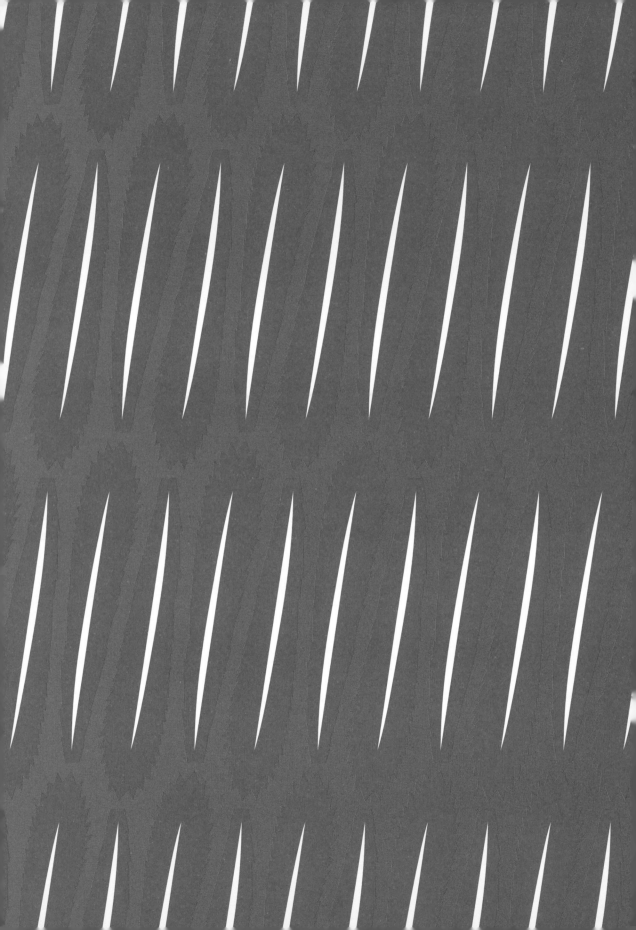

Eryngium foetidum

Culantro

Named Eryngium *– Greek for 'sea holly' – on account of its spikiness, and* foetidum *– 'stinky odour' – because of its smell, this is a native of many Caribbean islands and Southeast Asia.*

GROW
Culantro grows best in well-drained soil in part shade. The more shade it has, the bigger and more pungent its leaves will be.

EAT WITH
Peppers, tomatoes, garlic, lime, basil, yogurt, noodles, rice, chicken, pork, beef, seafood.

TRY
Pulse a large bunch of culantro in a food processor with salt, garlic, lime juice and green chilli to taste, then gradually add enough olive oil to make a dressing. Serve with chicken or seafood.

HEAL
Culantro root has traditionally been eaten raw for scorpion stings. It is used in India to alleviate stomach pains. In traditional medicine, it has been prescribed to help fever, chills, vomiting and diarrhoea. The leaves can be eaten in a chutney to stimulate the appetite.

ALTHOUGH A COUSIN of coriander (which is also sometimes called cilantro), culantro is very much its own herb, known as *shado beni* in Trinidad, *recao* in Puerto Rico and *man dhonia* in India. It can be used to replace coriander, although in reduced quantities, owing to its greater pungency.

Rich in calcium, iron, carotene and riboflavin, culantro is used widely in Latin American, Caribbean, Thai and Malaysian cooking, particularly in soups, noodle dishes and curries. It is a component of a Puerto Rican salsa made with tomatoes, garlic, onion, lemon juice and chillies and served with tortilla chips. There's also sofrito, the secret ingredient in many Latin Caribbean recipes. This flavour base for soups and stews is made from very finely chopped garlic, onion, green pepper, coriander and culantro leaves, sweated in oil until soft and aromatic.

Eyebright

Found in Europe, North America and western and northern Asia, eyebright was used by the original botanist – and student of Plato and Aristotle – Theophrastus.

GROW
Preferring moist soil, eyebright grows well in light, sandy soils with partial shade.

TRY
Pour boiling water over fresh or dried eyebright and infuse for ten minutes to make eyebright tea. You can also use this as a compress on tired or sore eyes.

HEAL
Eyebright is famous for its use in treating eye problems, including slowing down age-related progressive vision weakness – although do seek expert help with this. Eyebright can also reduce mucus discharge during colds and flu. A home remedy of eyebright mixed with ground mace and fennel seeds – drunk with juice – can apparently help to counter memory loss.

A FEW HUNDRED YEARS later, Dioscorides, author of one of the original medical herbals, the first-century *De Materia Medica*, used it while he accompanied the Roman legions on their numerous trips around Europe. And there's more: eyebright was a fourteenth-century cure for 'all evils of the eye'; an eyebright ale was described during the reign of Queen Elizabeth I; and Milton writes of Adam having his eyes cleaned with eyebright, 'for he had much to see'. Eyebright was commonly employed in European folk medicine for all kinds of eye-related ailment. It is easy to see why the botanical name – coming from one of the Greek Graces, Euphrosyne – means 'gladness'.

Growing 20 cm (8 in.) tall, with oval, jagged-edged leaves and white or purple blooms with yellow variegations, eyebright is a member of the figwort family. There are hundreds of different kinds. The whole above-ground plant – stems, leaves and flowers – is edible, though slightly bitter, and contains vitamins B, C, E and beta-carotene, antioxidants and flavonoids (the last being good for poor memory).

Eutrema wasabi

Wasabi

---

*With a fierce, burning smell and a sharp, cleansing taste,
wasabi is a herbaceous perennial that grows naturally
in cold mountain streams in Japan.*

GROW
Grow in a humid, shady place
in boggy soil (it must not
dry out). Wasabi loves cool,
cloudy summers.

EAT WITH
Fish, seafood, smoked fish,
beef, chicken, avocado, peas,
potatoes, rice.

TRY
Make a simple sauce by
stirring 1 teaspoon wasabi
paste into 200 g (7 oz)
fromage frais, Greek yogurt
or whipped cream, adding
lemon juice and a pinch of
sugar to taste. Serve with
beef or smoked fish.

HEAL
Wasabi can clear the sinuses,
fight off bacterial infection
and reduce the risk of
cardiovascular disease,
while its high levels of
antioxidants can boost
the immune system.

WHAT LOOKS LIKE a root or rhizome is in fact the stem of the plant, with the characteristic leaf scars where old leaves have fallen off or been collected. Sometimes called Japanese horseradish – and indeed it can be swapped for horseradish – wasabi is difficult to cultivate. Outside Japan, it is hard to find fresh wasabi plants, but do look out for some pioneering growers. The plant takes two years to reach maturity and is highly perishable, so it is expensive to ship far from its growing patch.

The burning sensation associated with eating wasabi is not oil-based, and so it is short-lived compared to the effects of chilli peppers. Depending on the quantity that has been consumed, they can still be painful, and generally affect the nasal passage. A group of chemists won an Ig Nobel Prize in 2011 for inventing a 'wasabi alarm' to wake deaf people, using wasabi's potent scent.

Associated mostly with fish dishes, particularly sushi and sashimi, whole wasabi stems are sold in tubs of water in Japan. It is readily available elsewhere as a pale green powder or paste, which is traditionally served in tiny quantities with sashimi, often mixed with soy sauce to taste for dipping. The paste is also used in sushi, sandwiched thinly between the fish and the rice.

But wasabi has uses beyond its traditional role accompanying raw fish. Try it instead of horseradish to give a fiery kick to beef; add it to that British favourite mushy peas to serve with fish and chips; or stir it into hollandaise sauce, but remember that a little goes a long way. If you can grow your own, wasabi's heart-shaped leaves and stems are both edible and can be added to salads for a spicy kick.

Filipendula ulmaria

Meadowsweet

This is the herb of pain relief: meadowsweet contains the key headache-busting ingredient used in aspirin.

GROW
Meadowsweet thrives in rich, moist soil and blooms well near water or in damp meadows. Prune if the leaves get tattered in the summer.

EAT WITH
Apples, peaches, strawberries, raspberries, gooseberries, sweetcorn, peas, asparagus, rice, cream.

TRY
Use meadowsweet leaves or flowers to infuse the custard when making strawberry ice cream; for a sorbet, macerate the berries with meadowsweet.

HEAL
An infusion of leaves and flowers can be taken for feverish colds or mild rheumatic pains or given to children for upset stomachs. Fluid extract can help with gastritis or chronic rheumatism. Avoid during pregnancy or if sensitive to aspirin.

MENTIONED IN GEOFFREY CHAUCER'S 'Knight's Tale', the first story in his *Canterbury Tales* (*c.* 1400), as meadwort, meadowsweet is a native of Europe and western Asia. It is now prevalent in North America, too, where its other names include the Queen of the Prairies. Also referred to as bridewort (it was strewn in churches for weddings and used in bridal garlands), the herb bears clusters of graceful creamy-white, almond-scented flowers and tall, erect stems.

Meadowsweet's wrinkled, dark-green leaves resemble those of the elm tree – *ulmaria* means 'elm-like' – and, like the bark of slippery elm, meadowsweet contains salicylic acid, which has long been used as a painkiller. In 1897 the German chemist Felix Hoffmann created a synthetic variant of salicin, derived from meadowsweet, which paved the way for aspirin. Indeed, aspirin was named after the old botanical name for meadowsweet: *Spiraea ulmaria*. Meadowsweet has long been considered beneficial to health: in the past it was used to treat arthritis, rheumatism and upset stomachs, and it is undoubtedly the herb for headaches. Given its sweet scent, it is well-known as a strewing herb – one that Queen Elizabeth I favoured for freshening her rooms.

Meadowsweet's distinctive sweet, almond flavour is much underused in the kitchen, although foraging chefs are beginning to appreciate its charms. The leaves can be added to salads and soups, while the flower heads can be used in the same way as those of elder (see page 176) – they make a particularly good cordial. Meadowsweet is a traditional flavouring for beer, mead and wine. Dried meadowsweet can be sprinkled over sweet and savoury dishes to add a hint of new-mown hay.

Foeniculum vulgare

Fennel

Tall and graceful, fennel is a perennial plant with a warm, liquorice-like aroma.

GROW
Plant fennel seeds after the last frost in deep, well-drained soil. Fennel is one for the back of your herb garden, and be aware that it grows a very long taproot. It will need staking in windier locations.

EAT WITH
Potatoes, onions, tomatoes, duck, pork, oily fish, shellfish, anchovies, chilli, olives, oranges, cream, Parmesan cheese.

TRY
Stuff fennel fronds into the cavities of fish before baking. Make a refreshing salad from wafer-thin slices of Florence fennel, orange segments, chopped red chilli, masses of fennel fronds and a little olive oil. Add fennel fronds to coleslaw. Scatter fennel flowers over soups and salads.

HEAL
Take an infusion of fennel seeds for indigestion and wind; an infusion of the plant can increase the flow of milk during breastfeeding. A fennel tincture can be used for constipation.

IT IS SAID that the town of Marathon in Greece, legendary as the origin of the long-distance race, was originally named thus because of an abundance of fennel (*maratho* means 'fennel' in Greek). Fennel is a dandyish plant with feathery fronds, thick, grey-green, bamboo-like stalks and yellow flower umbels (clusters of flowers in which stalks of nearly equal length spring from a common centre). Growing up to 1.8 m (6 ft) tall, it makes a distinctive addition to a wide herb border. The taste is fresh, sweet and aniseedy, adding a touch of spring to salads and sauces. We're talking here, of course, about the herb stems, flower head and seeds, rather than the much-loved bulb of the Florence fennel variety.

If you are lucky enough to find wild fennel in flower, pick the blossoms and dry them; you will have made a very fashionable (and expensive) ingredient sold as fennel pollen, sometimes called the spice of angels. Its flavour is remarkably intense. Just a sprinkling is enough to enhance pork, chicken, fish and vegetable dishes.

Fennel's liquorice notes mellow when it is cooked, partnering particularly well with fish. In Provence, red mullet is baked on a bed of fennel stems. Although it's not the easiest herb to find in the market, it's extremely straightforward to grow, as long as you give it lots of room. Come September, you can harvest the flavourful seeds from its umbelliferous flower heads.

Woodruff

The sixteenth-century herbalist John Gerard wrote of woodruff: 'It is reported to be put into wine, to make a man merry, and to be good for the heart and liver[;] it prevaileth in wounds.'

GROW
Plant in moist, well-drained soil in shade, as sun will damage the leaves. Woodruff can be invasive in the garden, but it can be grown in containers and works well as a houseplant.

EAT WITH
Chicken, rabbit, salad leaves, apples, melons, pears, strawberries.

TRY
Scatter woodruff flowers over salads or use them to garnish fruit drinks and wine cups.

HEAL
Make woodruff tea with a small handful of fresh leaves infused in boiling water for ten to fifteen minutes: use to soothe stomach aches and migraines, and combat insomnia. Bruised, the leaves can reduce swelling and encourage wounds to heal.

ALSO KNOWN AS master-of-the-wood, woodruff is an invigorating plant, with fragrant flowers and leaves giving off a persistent scent of freshly mown hay (one of its other names is, not surprisingly, new-mowed-hay). It is not an easy herb to cultivate, although it can be foraged from woodlands and orchards.

Woodruff has been used to cure everything from restlessness, insomnia and stomach ache to neuralgia and bladder stones, as well as respiratory conditions and haemorrhoids. Modern herbalists use it as a laxative and anti-arthritic, while a tea made from the leaves acts as a diuretic. Scatter woodruff at the back of your bookcase to lessen the musty smell of books kept over a long period of time.

The Germans love woodruff. In Berlin bars you can order a *Berliner Weisse mit Schuss,* a light beer with a shot of woodruff syrup. It is also commonly found in jelly form and added to Rhine wine to make a May Day punch, known as *Waldmeisterbowle* – a combination of white wine, brandy, champagne and fresh strawberries. This drink works equally well with lemonade for a child-friendly version.

Ginkgo

*What outlived the dinosaurs, has a life expectancy
of a thousand years and can survive a nuclear blast?*

GROW

Prepare the seeds by removing the pith (wearing gloves), then washing in mild detergent. Sow immediately in equal parts loam-based seed compost (seed starting mix) and horticultural grit. Germination takes four months; plant the seedlings in a container and grow there for four years; then, once a tree is planted in the garden, you just need to wait another twenty years to see if it fruits or not. Of course, you could always buy a small ginkgo tree and start from there – they are remarkably easy to care for.

HEAL

Ginkgo tablets, which are widely available, can be used for poor circulation, varicose veins and memory loss. A decoction of ginkgo can be used for persistent coughs and asthmatic conditions. Studies are also suggesting that ginkgo may help people with Alzheimer's disease improve thinking, perform daily activities and have fewer feelings of depression.

No joke: it's ginkgo, Darwin's 'living fossil', the hardy deciduous tree that is resistant to insects, fungi, viruses, pollution and nuclear radiation. Unsurprisingly, the maidenhair tree (its alternative name) is believed to imbue humans with similar superpowers: in Chinese medicine, ginkgo has been used to treat everything from asthma and coughs to stomach bugs and hangovers. It is even said to improve mental function, memory and reasoning, although the evidence for that is disputed.

The leaves of the ginkgo tree are used to make medicinal extracts. Ginkgo means 'silver apricot' in Chinese, referring to the fruit (*biloba* means 'two-lobed', on account of the split in the middle of the fan-shaped leaves). The fruit is round, plum-sized and brown, with very little flesh covering the 'nut'; the Chinese tend to let it rot off before using the nuts. There is some debate about whether it is safe to eat them raw, and, more often than not, they are roasted or cooked in soups or stir-fries (or, in Japan, in savoury custards). They are also painted red – the colour of happiness – and hung up at weddings. In Japan, where ginkgo is treated as a deity (there is a 3,500-year-old specimen in the Di Lin Temple at Fu Lai Mountain), six trees survived the atomic bomb in Hiroshima, so it is regarded there as the 'bearer of hope'.

Houttuynia

—

Invasive but pretty, this Japanese native is a water-loving herb that is widely used in Southeast Asian cooking, and pretty much unknown anywhere else.

GROW
Houttuynia is tolerant of a wide range of soils, from dry to wet, in shade or in sun, and is a good plant to grow in containers, where its spread can be restricted.

EAT WITH
Beef, duck, fish, seafood, coriander, garlic, lemongrass, mint, nasturtium.

TRY
Shred the leaves into clear soups. Add them to vegetable stir-fries and seafood dishes. Deep-fry the leaves in tempura batter.

HEAL
A lotion can be used on cuts and grazes; a syrup can ease coughs; and drinking what in Japan is called *dokudami cha* – an infusion of the fresh herb – one day a month can act as a general detoxifier.

ALSO CALLED HEARTLEAF (its red-edged leaves are heart-shaped), houttuynia's Chinese name means 'fishy-smell herb' – which is fair enough, given that its coriander aroma has fish and citrus notes. In Vietnam it is also known as fish mint. Japanese houttuynia has more orange and coriander aromas than the Chinese type, and so is more appetising to some.

A herbaceous perennial plant, growing to between 20 and 80 cm (8–30 in.), houttuynia thrives in wet soil and even enjoys having its feet in water in full sun. You can harvest the leaves from spring to autumn, breaking a couple in your hands first to check the aroma. The cultivar 'Chameleon' – also known as court jester – has beautiful orange-yellow-green leaves. Houttuynia is a love-it-or-hate-it kind of herb, though, so one person's stink could well be another's perfume.

In Japan, houttuynia is called *dokudami*, or 'poison-blocking plant', referring to its use in herbal medicine for its antiviral and antibacterial properties. It is also known to work for hay fever and poor circulation, and has recently been suggested to have anti-obesity properties.

Humulus lupulus

Hops

*A bine rather than a vine (it twines clockwise around
its support), the hop is the herb of beer and sleep.*

GROW
If you are not near a
community hop-growing
project (they can be found in
some cities), buy hop plants
or rhizomes from a disease-
free source. Hops prefer
deep, well-drained loam
and plenty of sun, with
room to climb.

EAT WITH
Fish, eggs, soft cheese,
tomatoes, rice, pasta.

TRY
Blanch hop shoots and/
or leaves in boiling water,
then drain very thoroughly.
Heat gently with butter and
seasoning. Use in omelettes,
risottos and pasta dishes.

HEAL
Hops can relieve aches and
pains and kill bacteria, as
well as encourage a good
night's sleep. Take as a tea
(combine with valerian –
page 205 – for extra effect),
as a tincture or as tablets or
lotion.

HOPPING STRAIGHT TO the name, *Humulus* probably comes
from humus – the rich, moist ground in which the plant grows best –
while *lupulus* is from *lupus*, Latin for 'wolf'. As Pliny explained, when
grown among osiers (a kind of willow), the hops strangle them as
a wolf might a sheep. The word hop itself comes from the Anglo-
Saxon *hoppan*, 'to climb'.

The root of this perennial is stout; the stem reaches a great
length and is tough, flexible and notably prickly; and the leaves
are heart-shaped and dark green with finely toothed edges. The
flowers spring from the axils of the leaves. Hops are dioecious, from
the Greek meaning 'two households' – in other words, they have
separate male and female plants. It's the unpollinated flowers of
the female plant that are harvested for beer. The flowers are leafy,
cone-like catkins called strobiles, from which is derived much of
the lupulin that gives hops their characteristic bitter taste.

The Romans were hot on hops: they would eat the young
shoots in spring. Millennia later, those young shoots are back in
fashion; they were recently labelled the most expensive vegetable in
the world, at €1,000 a kilo. Also known as hop asparagus, the shoots
are in fact closer to samphire in texture and are increasingly being
used by imaginative chefs.

Thanks to the chemical methylbutenol, mildly sedative hops
are helpful for a good night's sleep. Hop tea is recommended for
insomnia and restlessness and to stimulate the appetite, while a hop
pillowcase can aid rest: just sprinkle hops with alcohol and slip them
into your pillow.

Hypericum perforatum

St John's Wort

If you tread on St John's wort after sundown, you will be swept up on the back of a magic horse that will charge around until sunrise before depositing you on open ground. Apparently.

GROW

To help seeds to germinate, soak them in warm water for a few hours or overnight before sowing. St John's wort will crowd out other plants, so you might consider growing it in a pot first, then burying the pot in the garden to keep it under control.

HEAL

An infusion of the plant can be used to soothe anxiety, irritability and nervous tension as well as to bathe wounds and skin sores. Tablets can be taken for mild to moderate depression and other related illnesses, including seasonal affective disorder and obsessive–compulsive disorder. Always check with a doctor.

WITH STALKLESS LEAVES and cheery yellow, scented flowers, this herbaceous perennial grows freely in woodlands, hedges, meadows and roadsides. The Latin name comes from the Greek *hyperikon*, meaning 'over apparition' or 'almost over ghosts': it was believed the herb was so obnoxious to evil spirits that even a whiff of it would cause them to vanish. *Perforatum* refers to the black dots found on the leaves and flowers, which – although they look like little black holes – are in fact tiny glands that release those essential plant oils and resins. It gets its common name, St John's wort, from the fact that the brightly coloured flowers usually open on John the Baptist's birthday, 24 June. Indeed, St John's wort is one of the so-called St John's herbs – which also include yarrow (page 12), mugwort (page 45), fennel (page 93) and elder (page 176); they would be picked on St John's birthday and hung over doors and windows to keep evil spirits away. Meanwhile, so-called St John's fires would be lit on hills and high places to scare away heavenly fire and supernatural malice at the time of the year when crops were coming to maturity.

Nowadays, the herb of St John is used by millions of people to ward off that other kind of spirit: depression. It has been shown by some studies to be as effective as drugs such as Prozac, but without their side effects, thanks to active ingredients that include hypericin and hyperforum. Although the results are inconclusive, it is thought that St John's wort boosts and maintains the feel-good hormone serotonin. However, as ever, do consult your doctor if you plan to take it.

Hyssop

A favourite herb of honeybees, bumblebees and digger bees – it's even used in making honey – hyssop is also the herb of purification: 'Purge me with Hyssop, and I shall be clean' (Psalms 51:7).

GROW

Sow in early spring and make sure it gets as much sun as possible. If you don't have success with seeds, it's probably easier to grow from cuttings.

EAT WITH

Apricots, peaches, plums, cherries, cranberries, beetroot, cabbage, mushrooms, tomatoes, winter squash, carrots, eggs, game, lamb.

TRY

Add a teaspoon of chopped hyssop leaf to Yorkshire pudding batter. Drop a couple of sprigs into a pan of poached peaches, apricots or plums. Add chopped hyssop to the batter when making cornmeal muffins or cornbread. Include hyssop leaves in a game pie or casserole.

HEAL

Half a cup of hot hyssop infusion every couple of hours can encourage sweating at the start of a cold or flu. Hyssop syrup is useful for coughs. Hyssop is not for everyone; always consult a doctor.

HYSSOP IS A handsome, bushy plant, with clusters of deep-blue flowers and dark evergreen leaves. Used sparingly, it can lift a dish with aplomb, thanks to its exhilaratingly minty aroma and potent, bitter taste. The leaves can be added to salads, as can the flowers, or included in soups and stews. Besides being paired with rich foods such as game and lamb – it can help with digestion – hyssop is wonderful in sweet things like sorbets and fruit pies. Hyssop tea, a traditional remedy for colds, is made by pouring boiling water over crushed dried hyssop leaves and infusing for fifteen minutes.

Hyssop grows wild in the hot stone walls and arid banks of southern Europe and northern Africa. It is an evergreen, so you can pick the leaves at any time. Given its enjoyable scent, it makes a lovely container plant and works well in shared outdoor spaces.

Bay

———

'Tis thought the king is dead; we will not stay.
The bay trees in our country are all wither'd
And meteors fright the fixed stars of heaven.

WILLIAM SHAKESPEARE, RICHARD II

GROW
Grow bay in a sheltered, sunny position; it is happy as a container plant and can be moved indoors during winter. Pick the leaves throughout the year.

EAT WITH
Beef, chicken, lamb, pork, game, fish, chestnuts, tomatoes, potatoes, lentils, rice, orange, lemon, plums, figs, cream.

TRY
Infuse the cream for pannacotta or custard with a fresh bay leaf. Put a bay leaf in the dish when making rice pudding. Add to a dried fruit compote or to autumn fruits poached in red wine. Tuck a few leaves into the cavity of a whole fish before roasting.

HEAL
Bay essential oil can be massaged onto sprains and used to relieve headaches. Added to food, bay leaves can reduce flatulence. An infusion of bay leaves can promote sweating at the start of colds and flu. A herbal tea made with bay can treat digestive disorders.

ACCORDING TO MYTH, the bay tree was born of unrequited love. Apollo, struck by one of Eros' lust-laden arrows, chased after the nymph Daphne, who by all accounts did not reciprocate his interest. Running into the woods, she begged her father, the river god Peneus, to save her. Her wish was his command, and he turned her into a bay tree. Apollo's love was unabated and he kept her forever, wearing her special glossy leaves around his head on grand occasions. The bay wreath became the highest honour that could be bestowed on poets, hence the apex of a job title: poet laureate (laureate means crowned with bay).

Native to the eastern Mediterranean, the bay we know and love in our kitchens has long been cultivated in northern Europe and America for its sweet, balsamic aroma and notes of nutmeg. Whether bundled up in a classic bouquet garni with thyme and parsley or used on its own, fresh or dried, the bay leaf is indispensable for flavouring stocks, stews, sauces and soups. It is equally at home added to the water when boiling potatoes or threaded onto barbecue skewers between chunks of fish, meat or vegetables. Bay is classically used to infuse the milk for a béchamel sauce; less familiar is the old custom of adding it to custards and other sweet, milky dishes. If cooking with fresh leaves, crush or rub them before use to release their aromatic compounds; crumble or grind dried leaves as you need them.

Lavender

Hide it in your trousseau, lady fair.
Let its lovely fragrance flow
Over you from head to toe,
Lightening on your eyes, your cheek, your hair.

CUMBERLAND CLARK, THE FLOWER SONG BOOK, 1929

GROW
Lavender flourishes in dry, well-drained, sandy or gravelly soil in full sun.

EAT WITH
Blackberries, strawberries, apricots, peaches, plums, figs, lamb, rabbit, duck, white fish, orange, lemon, white chocolate, goat's cheese, walnuts, almonds, thyme, oregano, rosemary.

TRY
Infuse melted white chocolate with lavender flowers, strain and use in desserts or to make truffles. Make lavender sugar by grinding the flowers with a little caster (superfine) sugar, then transfer to a jar, top up with more sugar and seal. Use in baking. You can do likewise with salt for a savoury rub for meat.

HEAL
Smelling lavender is good for headaches. A tincture of lavender sprinkled on a pillow, or a cup of lavender tisane, can promote relaxation and sleep. Essential oil of lavender can be added to a bottle of water and sprayed on sunburn for relief.

A GREY-LEAVED, ROUNDED bush with fragrant flower spikes, lavender is a staple in all kinds of garden. The herbalist Nicholas Culpeper declined even to describe it, since it 'is so well known, being an inhabitant of almost every garden'. Different kinds of lavender include *Lavandula angustifolia* (common or English lavender), *L. latifolia* (spike lavender) and *L. stoechas* (French or Spanish lavender). Each has its own twist, although the English is softest on the nose.

Lavender, of course, is predominantly known for its aroma and is principally used in perfumery, but its flowers and leaves also have a role to play in the kitchen. It grows widely in Mediterranean countries, particularly in Provence, where you will find vast swathes of purple lavender fields in summer. A good starting point in cooking is to pair it with the foods of those regions. It is particularly lovely with summer fruits such as apricots and peaches, and makes a wonderful ice cream or crème brûlée. It works surprisingly well with fish, and meats such as lamb, rabbit and game, too (no surprise, given the way its aromatic neighbours, rosemary and thyme, are used). Try adding a little lavender to a marinade for lamb or chicken, or rubbing it into the meat with salt, other scented herbs and a little olive oil. Use in moderation, since it can dominate. The leaves are milder than the flowers; try adding a few to savoury stews.

Levisticum officinale

Lovage

———

Lovage – from the German Liebstöckel, *literally 'love stick' – has been lovingly grown in Europe since Roman times.*

GROW
A hardy perennial, lovage is easy to grow from seed, or you could buy a pot and plant it on. It's a thirsty plant, so keep the soil moist.

EAT WITH
Tomatoes, peas, beans, lentils, carrots, potatoes, leeks, lettuce, cucumbers, ham, chicken, smoked fish, white fish, cheese.

TRY
Add a few leaves of lovage to pea soup or leek and potato soup to give a delicate curry flavour and aroma. Use finely chopped young lovage in a dressing for cucumber or in a cucumber sandwich. Add chopped lovage to a tomato sauce.

HEAL
A decoction of the roots can aid indigestion, cystitis, gout and painful menstruation. Gargle the decoction for mouth ulcers and tonsillitis. Chew the seeds to relieve flatulence. Do not take if you are pregnant or have kidney problems.

A MEMBER OF THE Umbelliferae family, lovage is the tall uncle of parsley (page 159), growing to a whopping 2.5 m (8 ft) high. The family connection is clear to see, given its resemblance to the flat-leaf variety of parsley, although lovage leaves are larger and darker. Lovage can be swapped for parsley in cooking, but the flavour will be warmer and spicier. It can also be substituted for herb celery (see page 36); indeed, the French sometimes call lovage *céleri bâtard*, or 'false' celery.

Strongly aromatic, with notes of parsley, celery, anise and curry, lovage is well worth growing. It is very handy in the kitchen, but be aware that a little can go a long way. Just a leaf or two will add flavour to salads, stocks, soups and casseroles. The thicker stalks can be peeled and blanched, then dressed in vinaigrette, while the seeds are sometimes ground and used as a seasoning. If you grow your own lovage, the root can be cooked in the same way as celeriac. The home cook and food writer Nigella Lawson adores lovage. In her book *How To Eat* (1998), she writes about adding the herb – almost without thinking about it – to a shepherd's pie or thick soup. She grew her lovage from seed before planting it out; 'now each spring it grows back huge, its bushy, long-stalked arms outstretched, magnificently architectural.'

As a medicinal herb, lovage has been recommended as a cure for rheumatism, sore throat and indigestion. In medieval times, a cordial was made from the leaves. Travellers also slipped lovage leaves into their shoes as a form of foot deodorizer.

Limnophila aromatica

Rice Paddy Herb

Grown in the flooded rice paddies of Southeast Asia during the wet season, rice paddy herb, with its whorls of three long leaves along a thick stem, is a tropical flowering plant in the plantain family.

GROW
The easiest way is to find someone who has a plant (try a Thai or Vietnamese grocer) and get fresh stems from them. Place the stems in water and cover with a plastic bag to ensure humidity; this essentially creates a mini greenhouse. When enough roots have formed for your liking, plant in soil.

EAT WITH
Coconut milk, fish, noodles, shallots, green vegetables, root vegetables, lemongrass, coriander, lime.

TRY
Scatter coarsely chopped rice paddy herb over sweet-and-sour fish soups.

HEAL
An infusion of rice paddy herb can be used to soothe a fever and lessen mucus. The aroma of the leaves is refreshing and relaxing.

THE VIETNAMESE ARE probably the biggest users of rice paddy herb (also known as finger grass), adding it to vegetable soups, fish dishes and *canh chua* – a sour soup based on a tamarind-flavoured broth. It was introduced to North America in the 1970s as a result of Vietnamese immigration after the Vietnam War.

The herb's name hints at its natural habitat: *Limnophila* literally means 'lover of ponds'. With an attractive flowery, lemony scent and a pungent cumin-cum-lemon flavour, rice paddy herb is fragrant and delicate, and goes well with coriander (cilantro) and lemongrass. Its taste has been described as reminiscent of the air after a violent summer thunderstorm.

Honeysuckle

_____

Honeysuckle: historically, for hiccoughs.

GROW
Climbing honeysuckles, such as *Lonicera caprifolium*, prefer fertile, moist, well-drained soil, with the top growth in full sun. Dense, shrubby honeysuckles, such as *L. nitida*, also need well-drained soil.

TRY
Make honeysuckle syrup: put a couple of handfuls of honeysuckle flowers in a bowl and pour over enough boiling water to cover. Leave overnight, then strain. Measure the water and heat with an equal volume of sugar, stirring until the sugar has dissolved. Simmer for two to three minutes, then cool. Use in drinks or drizzle over fruit, ice creams, sorbets and cakes.

HEAL
Tea made from honeysuckle flowers, with a little honey added, can boost the immune system and soothe headaches. The aromatherapy oil extracted from the sweet-smelling shrub can alleviate mental and physical stress. Take note: the berries are poisonous.

ALSO, NATURALLY, THE scent of summer evenings. This deciduous, perennial climber is commonly found growing along walls or scrambling through trees and hedgerows. With pale-green, oval leaves and pink-tinged, creamy-white, tubular flowers, it is exceptionally pretty, although the berries are poisonous. The bitter leaves were once the favourite food of goats – hence the name of one variety, *Lonicera caprifolium*, meaning 'goat leaf'. There are 180 species of honeysuckle – 100 in China and the rest native to India, Europe and North America. The botanical name, *Lonicera*, stems from the Renaissance botanist Adam Lonitzer, who wrote a book of herbs, *Kräuterbuch*, in 1557.

Honeysuckle has a long history of health promotion. It was recommended by Pliny to be taken with wine for spleen disorders, and listed in the *Tang Bencao* (the key text used for traditional Chinese medicine) in 659 BC as one of the most important Chinese herbs for clearing the body of poison. The sixteenth-century herbalist John Gerard grew honeysuckle in his garden and used it to cure 'the hicket' (hiccoughs). It is known to have a high level of vitamin C and the anti-inflammatory agent quercetin.

Lemon Balm

*With its square stems and leaves in pairs, it looks like mint,
yet tastes like lemon. This self-seeding bee attractor (*melissa
*is Greek for bee) has a lingering lemony scent and a long
history of medicinal use.*

GROW
Lemon balm can grow up to
75 cm (2½ ft) tall. Like mint,
it tends to ramble and grows
equally well in the garden or
in a container, as long as it
is in decent soil, away from
excessive heat and given
plenty of water.

EAT WITH
Apricots, figs, strawberries,
melon, carrots, mushrooms,
fennel, tomatoes, white
cheese, pork, chicken, fish.

TRY
Mix finely chopped lemon
balm with softened butter
and insert under the skin of
a chicken before roasting,
for a delicate lemony flavour.
Make lemon balm water: fill
a jug or pitcher with lemon
balm leaves, add a thinly
sliced lemon and fill up with
ice-cold water.

HEAL
An infusion of fresh or
dried leaves can help with
indigestion, nausea and
nervous exhaustion; use
a lemon balm cream on
insect bites; and use lemon
balm massage oil to relieve
tension and non-severe
depression.

ALTHOUGH UNDERAPPRECIATED IN the garden, lemon balm is very easy to grow and highly resistant to disease. The essential oil in the plant is valued by aromatherapists, who consider it to be uplifting and calming. It is sometimes added to skincare products as an anti-inflammatory.

Lemon balm has traditionally been used for such diverse conditions as hair loss, depression and headaches. Small trials show it to have antiviral and antioxidant properties. No evidence is required for the efficacy of a cup of lemon balm tea on an early summer's evening, or indeed a glass of lemon balm wine, which was believed by the seventeenth-century diarist and gardener John Evelyn to 'comfort the heart and [drive] away melancholy and sadness'.

When cooking, choose the younger, more tender leaves from the top of the plant. The lemony scent means it can be used anywhere you would use lemon: in butter sauces for fish or chicken, in stuffings, salads, salsas and desserts, and for infusing creams and custards, too.

Mint

Before F. Scott Fitzgerald's novel The Great Gatsby *(1925) unfolds as it inevitably must, the main characters consider a cool herb in a heated moment.*

GROW

Mints are easy to grow: they can thrive on scrubland, so this is a great herb to start nurturing if you are new to gardening. Growing it in pots prevents it from spreading. Chop it back regularly – the smaller, newer leaves are the mintiest. Grow different varieties apart to avoid hybridization.

EAT WITH

Potatoes, peas, cucumber, tomatoes, peppers, carrots, feta cheese, pineapple, strawberries, figs, blackcurrants, blueberries, chocolate, lamb, duck, beef, couscous, rice, yogurt, garlic, chilli, lime, lemon, parsley, coriander (cilantro).

HERE'S DAISY: '"OPEN the whisky, Tom," she ordered, "and I'll make you a mint julep. Then you won't seem so stupid to yourself. . . Look at the mint!"' There is no other narrative detail to clarify exactly what it is about the mint that is worth looking at, nor any explanation of how mint can resolve stupidity. Indeed, this might not be the best herb to prescribe to the men in the room: mint had associations in ancient times with robbing soldiers of their courage and – according to Pliny – 'impeding generation by preventing seminal fluids from obtaining their requisite consistency'. However, Daisy might still be on to something: mint can heal upset stomachs and cleanse bad breath.

Mint is the common name of plants of the *Mentha* genus. There are hundreds of varieties – from pineapple mint to ginger mint to eau-de-cologne mint – but they come down to two basic categories: peppermint (see page 120) and spearmint (see page 122). The former is the one we use mostly in cooking, while the latter is more fiery, peppery and spicy, but with a cooling quality – better for drinking as a tea or using in desserts.

This versatile herb is a mainstay of cuisines ranging from Middle Eastern to Mexican, English to Italian, Greek to Vietnamese. Certain constants crop up: the combination of lamb and mint, for example, in English roast lamb and mint sauce and the kebabs of the Middle East; and mint, cucumber and yogurt in the Indian raita and the Greek tzatziki.

Peppermint

---

*The ancient Romans crowned themselves with peppermint
at their feasts; the philosopher Pliny had taught them that
it would stimulate their minds and souls.*

TRY
Make a peppermint tisane:
infuse a bunch of peppermint
leaves in boiled water for
about five minutes, then
strain. It can be drunk hot
or cool.

HEAL
Ease a blocked nose by
putting fresh peppermint
sprigs in a bowl of boiling
water. Take an infusion to
soothe indigestion, flatulence
and colds; some studies
show that peppermint
can help with irritable
bowel syndrome, too. Use
peppermint massage oil to
relieve aching muscles.

A HYBRID OF WATERMINT and spearmint, peppermint is
indigenous to Europe and the Middle East and is now widely
cultivated around the world. It was not always regarded as a hybrid;
the Swedish botanist and father of modern taxonomy, Carl Linnaeus,
referred to it as its own species in 1753, from specimens he found in
England. Being a hybrid, peppermint is usually sterile, producing no
seeds and spreading instead by its rhizomes. It will grow wherever
you plant it – and quickly.

Peppermint has smooth, square stems and fleshy, slightly fuzzy
roots. Its dark-green leaves have reddish veins and toothed margins.
The high menthol content – 40 per cent, compared with spearmint's
0.5 per cent – gives it its intensely minty flavour and aroma. This
makes it particularly good for teas, desserts and confectionery, such
as peppermint creams. The high menthol content also means that
herbalists find peppermint invaluable. Its uses include reducing
nausea and cold symptoms and soothing indigestion and irritable
bowel syndrome – hence the tradition of after-dinner mints to
freshen the breath and ease digestion.

One of the best and simplest uses of mint is to cram it into
a teapot and fill up with boiling water to make tea. In Morocco,
Chinese gunpowder tea and plenty of sugar are added and the
mixture simmered briefly to strengthen the flavour.

Spearmint

———

*With pointed leaf tips giving the herb its 'spear', spearmint
is native to much of Europe and Asia, and has become
naturalized everywhere from Africa to the Americas.*

TRY
To make a mint julep, boil
100 g (3½ oz) sugar with
50 ml (2 fl. oz) water,
stirring to dissolve. Add six
spearmint sprigs and leave
to cool, then strain. Put a
tablespoon of the syrup into
a chilled glass and muddle
with a mint leaf. Fill up with
crushed ice, pour in a double
measure of bourbon and
stir well. Add a mint sprig
to serve.

ALSO KNOWN AS garden mint, Mary's herb and sage of
Bethlehem, spearmint plants grow anything up to 1 m (3 ft) in
height, with dark-green, deeply veined, serrated leaves. Their thick,
square stems – a famous trait of the mint family – are sometimes
hairy, sometimes not, and the small, purple, tubular flowers – similar
to peppermint's – grow in spikes of whorls. The herb has been used
medicinally for relieving headaches and stress, curing flatulence
and resolving hiccoughs (it relaxes the stomach muscles). Famously,
spearmint makes great toothpaste and breath-freshening chewing
gum, and it can also be mixed with yogurt to make a face pack.

Because spearmint contains only a little of the essential oil,
menthol, it is less pungent than many mints, making it the preferred
mint for cooking. Although peppermint (see page 120) is the one
most often used for mint tea, a spearmint tisane is pleasurable in its
own subtle way.

Mentha suaveolens 'Variegata'

Pineapple Mint

———

Pineapple mint is a cultivar of apple mint, a native of southern Europe and the western Mediterranean region.

TRY
Add chopped pineapple mint to a pineapple upside-down cake. After baking, drizzle a pineapple mint-flavoured syrup over the cake, if you like, or serve with thick yogurt mixed with chopped pineapple mint and icing (confectioners') sugar to taste.

GROWING ANYTHING FROM 40 to 100 cm (1⅓–3 ft) tall, butterfly-attracting pineapple mint bears small, purple, densely spiked flowers and bumpy, furry green leaves with creamy white margins. It has a distinctive fruity, minty, tropical aroma that really makes it stand out from the *Mentha* crowd.

Favouring damp conditions, pineapple mint is often grown as an ornamental plant, but it can be used in the kitchen in any recipe that calls for mint. It works well with its namesake in fruit salads or salsas, and is fantastic in a mojito or sorbet.

Micromeria

—————

*Deriving its name from the Greek words for 'small' (*micros*)
and 'portion' (*meris*), micromeria is a genus of dwarf shrubs,
widespread across the Mediterranean, East Africa, North
America and parts of Asia.*

GROW
Grow from seed in loamy,
well-drained soil in pots or in
the garden. Pick the leaves
from spring to late summer.

TRY
Micromeria fruticosa
makes a refreshing tea.
M. thymifolia can be used
in place of thyme for its
warmly aromatic notes; try
it in soups and stuffings,
with roasted vegetables and
meats, or with tomatoes
and soft cheese.

HEAL
Micromeria tea is claimed to
lower high blood pressure
and relieve insomnia, stress
and chronic digestion
difficulties.

BUSHY MICROMERIAS – a member of the Lamiaceae (formerly Labiatae) family – are small but beautifully formed. Their rounded, compact leaves can be used in cooking and in herbal teas, representing as they do a delicate take on more traditional herb flavours such as thyme and mint. There are plenty to choose from: from *Micromeria acropolitana* in Greece (presumed extinct but rediscovered in 2006) through to *M. weilleri*, found in Morocco. Some varieties have been used medicinally. *M. chamissonis*, for example, known as *yerba buena*, meaning 'good herb', can be made into an infusion to help with insomnia, colds and fever, and a decoction has also been used as an aphrodisiac.

A commonly available subspecies of micromeria, known as emperor's mint or Roman mint, is a native of Italy. Legend has it that it was found flourishing among the ruins of Emperor Hadrian's summer villa near Rome. Its small, rounded, greyish-green leaves are highly fragrant, and it makes a wonderful tea. Try it for flavouring egg- or tomato-based dishes, as well.

Bergamot

———

Often confused with bergamia, a European citrus fruit that is one of the flavourings of Earl Grey tea, bergamot – also known as horsemint and bee balm – is a beautiful wild plant native to North America.

GROW
Too tall for a window box, bergamot can be grown in a large pot in a shady place, or directly in the garden. Keep the soil moist.

EAT WITH
Pork, chicken, duck, fish, citrus fruits, strawberries, apples.

TRY
Add bergamot leaves and flowers to green salads or fruit salads. Make a salsa to accompany grilled fish by mixing finely chopped bergamot and parsley with diced orange segments. Make your own Oswego tea by adding fresh bergamot leaves to a pot of tea – you can add the leaves to wine or lemonade, too.

HEAL
An infusion can help with fever, colds, tight chests, coughs, nausea and digestive problems.

WITH FLAMBOYANT SCARLET, pink, white or purple flowers and oval green leaves with red veins, bergamot is understandably confused with the fruit, given its citrus aroma – although some liken its scent and flavour to oregano instead. Bergamot derives its Latin name from the sixteenth-century Spanish botanist and physician Nicolás Monardes, the son of an Italian bookseller and author of the first American herbal, *Joyfull Newes out of the New Found Worlde* (1577). Although he never travelled to America, Monardes was able to write about its herbs, trees and plants because he was a native of Seville, an important centre of navigation and commerce at the time.

Bergamot is also known as Oswego tea, because wild or purple bergamot grows around the Oswego River near Lake Ontario. Native Americans in the region once used it for its high levels of thymol, a powerful antiseptic that can relieve colds and bronchial complaints. After the Boston Tea Party of 1773, when colonists protesting Britain's tax on tea dumped a shipment into the harbour, Oswego tea temporarily replaced Indian tea.

Young bergamot leaves are wonderful shredded into green salads and fruit salads; it is best not to use the herb once the leaves become coarse and hairy. You can add the dried flowers and leaves to potpourri.

Myrrhis odorata

Sweet Cicely

One of nature's sweeteners, sweet cicely is a much underrated, must-have perennial.

GROW
Sow sweet cicely seeds in autumn – they need the winter to germinate – or grow in pots from April. This is a self-seeder, so watch out (and remove seeds as they form, if you don't want the plant to take over).

EAT WITH
Apricots, gooseberries, peaches, rhubarb, strawberries, cucumber, broad (fava) beans, tomatoes, courgettes, chicken, seafood, eggs, soft cheese.

TRY
Add sweet cicely to fish steaks baked *en papillote*, together with a splash of white wine, or use to stuff the cavities of whole fish before baking or barbecuing. Stir sweet cicely into a shellfish risotto towards the end of cooking.

HEAL
Infuse finely chopped ginger and sweet cicely in boiled water to make a tisane that can aid digestion.

NOT TO BE confused with hemlock, which it resembles, sweet cicely looks enchanting in gardens and woodlands, with its soft, lacy, fern-like leaves that appear very early in spring, giving frosty fingers something to harvest. Its beautiful, distinctive white flowers make a wonderful contribution to any herb garden, with their sweet liquorice smell – hence *odorata*, meaning 'scented'. In the past, sweet cicely was used by herbalists to treat coughs and flatulence, while a decoction of the roots was used for the bites of snakes and mad dogs. Taking a few sweet cicely seeds in a glass of hot milk before bedtime is said to treat insomnia.

With its honeyed, aniseedy notes, sweet cicely can be cooked with tart fruits such as rhubarb, gooseberries and apples to tone down their acidity: just add a handful of leaves to the pan and you won't need to use as much sugar. The flavour disappears with cooking, so add a little chopped cicely towards the end, too. Sweet cicely also works well in fruit salads and with cooling foods such as cucumber and green salad leaves. This gentle herb, so often paired with fruit, has a surprising affinity with shellfish, its anise flavour mimicking that classic partner for fish, pastis. The roots were traditionally cooked to serve as a vegetable or grated raw into salads, and they can also be made into a non-grape-based country wine.

You are unlikely to find sweet cicely in shops, but it is easy to grow and you'll be able to cut the leaves between spring and autumn.

Myrtle

———

The herb of love, myrtle is an evergreen shrub with small, shiny, oval leaves, scented white flowers and blue-black, juniper-like fruits.

GROW
Plant outdoors in late spring in a well-drained, sheltered position, planting out in a sheltered, sunny spot when established; or grow in a container and keep indoors in the winter.

EAT WITH
Fish, chicken, veal, venison, hare, wild boar, pork, lamb.

TRY
Myrtle leaves can be used in any recipe that calls for bay leaves (in addition to the bay). They are particularly good added towards the end of cooking roast lamb.

HEAL
Herbalists recommend myrtle essential oil for a variety of ailments, from wounds to wrinkles and impotence.

ALL PARTS OF luminescent myrtle are aromatic – from the sweet, orange-green leaves to the delicately scented, star-like flowers. Venus, the goddess of love, is famously showered in myrtle as she rises from the ocean in Botticelli's painting of the 1480s. This led to the custom of holding a wreath of myrtle over a bride's head during wedding ceremonies in many European countries. Queen Victoria got wind of it and ordered myrtle to be grown at Osborne House on the Isle of Wight – beginning a tradition of royal brides carrying myrtle sprigs at their weddings, still practised to this day.

Myrtle is best known in Italian cooking and in the Middle East, and is most often paired with fish, pork and game. The leaves are dried and used like bay leaves, and can also be preserved in olive oil or used fresh to flavour food when wood-smoking. The berries, too, can be dried, for use as a spice. They are perhaps best known for their role in seasoning mortadella sausages. Myrtle grows wild in Sardinia, where people often end a meal with a glass of mirto – a liqueur produced from either the berries (mirto rosso) or the leaves (mirto bianco).

Catnip

———

Also known as catmint, this is the famous (and harmless)
euphoria-inducing herb for cats.

GROW
Give catnip rich, well-drained soil, plenty of water and full sun, if possible. New plants can be small and delicate, so start seeds indoors in spring or, if outdoors, keep young plants under a protective mesh screen.

TRY
Make a sixteenth-century-style Italian salad with catnip, lettuce, mint, fennel, parsley, watercress, chervil, chicory and dandelion greens, flavoured with lots of salt, oil and vinegar. For catnip tea, infuse chopped fresh leaves in hot water. Combine with camomile or mint for an even more relaxing effect.

HEAL
Take an infusion to help colds, flu and indigestion. A catnip enema can be used to clear the colon. Apply catnip ointment to piles two or three times a day.

PET CATS ROLL around in it because bruising the herb releases its sweet and minty scent, which is caused by a chemical compound called nepetalactone. They go crazy for it, with much chewing, head-shaking and rolling around on the floor, and it's even been found to arouse sexual desire (we're still talking cats here). The size of the cat is said not to matter; catnip has a similar effect on jaguars, tigers, leopards and lions.

Catnip has been used for centuries as a relaxant for humans, too – particularly for overactive children. This rather gorgeous grey-green perennial, with square stems, terminal flower spikes and fuzzy, heart-shaped leaves, has been used to treat stomach complaints, as a pest repellent and to relieve stress and even arthritis, with herbalists preferring to use the flowering tops. Some studies suggest that catnip has mucilage properties, which makes it good for suppressing coughs: the mucilage coats the throat and soothes irritation. Catnip has even been smoked as a recreational drug. In the kitchen it's less commonly used – mostly in Italy – but it certainly makes an interesting guest herb in a salad. It is most often drunk as a tea.

Basil

___

Here we are in the land of kings. Basil is truly the king of herbs, its Latin name coming from the Greek word for 'king' or 'emperor', basileus.

GROW
Grow indoors on a sunny windowsill or outdoors in a sheltered, sunny position.

EAT WITH
Tomatoes, goat's cheese, mozzarella cheese, lemon, eggs, mint, shellfish, lamb, chicken, peaches, raspberries, strawberries, figs.

TRY
Tear a few basil leaves over fresh raspberries. Add a handful of basil leaves when making strawberry ice cream. Poach white peaches in sugar syrup with a handful of basil leaves, then serve with a little extra shredded basil.

HEAL
Scorpions in your brain aside, basil is said to have anti-inflammatory and antibacterial properties, and contains high levels of beta-carotene and vitamin A.

THIS TENDER, WARMLY spiced and peppery herb, with a hint of mint, has much by way of poetic, royal and religious connotation. In Portugal, on St John's and St Anthony's days (both in June), dwarf bush basil is traditionally presented in a pot with a poem and a pom-pom; the French call it *l'herbe royale*; and Keats wrote the long narrative poem 'Isabella, or the Pot of Basil' in 1818 on a subject that was taken up by several Pre-Raphaelite artists. Basil was said to have sprung up beneath the Cross on which Christ was crucified, and consequently it is used to sprinkle holy water in the Greek Orthodox Church. In India, where it is sacred to Vishnu and Krishna, basil is found in most Hindu homes. Apparently it provides protection against the lethal gaze of that fabulous beast, the basilisk.

There are mixed messages when it comes to basil's health benefits: according to Nicholas Culpeper, the French physician Hilarius thought that smelling too much basil would make you breed scorpions in your brain; the seventeenth-century English herbalist William Salmon, on the other hand, said that basil juice was good for 'Heart Qualms or Swooning Fits'.

Basil was originally cultivated 3,000 years ago in India, the Middle East and some Pacific Islands, and came to western Europe with the spice traders in the sixteenth century. Of course, we now know and love it as the quintessential summer herb, that great interlocutor between tomato and buffalo mozzarella, and the main constituent of the Italian pesto and the French pistou. This heady, fragrant herb has endless culinary uses and repays a certain amount of experimentation in the kitchen.

Ocimum basilicum 'Horapha'

Thai Basil

*A basil native to Southeast Asia, this sturdy variety is widely
used for its anise, clove and liquorice-like flavour.*

TRY
Add Thai basil to beef or
chicken stir-fries. Use it in a
mango salsa: mix with finely
diced red onion and chilli,
diced mango and lime juice.

WITH SMALL, NARROW, SHINY purple-veined leaves, purple
stems and pinkish flowers, Thai basil grows to a handsome 45 cm
(18 in.). It is much used in the curries of Thailand, Vietnam, Laos
and Cambodia, especially those based on coconut milk. It is also
an essential addition to the Vietnamese noodle soup pho, and a
key ingredient in the popular Taiwanese dish *sanbeiji*, or 'three-cup
chicken', made with soy sauce, rice wine and sesame oil.

Thai basil is not to be confused with Thai holy basil (*Ocimum
tenuiflorum*), which is known in India as tulsi. On the Indian
subcontinent, holy basil is used widely as a medicinal plant and
herbal tea, as well as playing an important role in the Vaishnava
tradition in Hinduism: devotees perform worship involving holy
basil plants or leaves.

Ocimum basilicum var. *purpurascens*

Dark Opal Basil

With leaves fit for royalty, and a soothing liquorice taste, this slower-growing variety of basil is well worth the wait.

EAT WITH
Tomatoes, goat's cheese, mozzarella cheese, soft cheese, rice, lemon, eggs, mint, shellfish, lamb, chicken, peaches, raspberries, strawberries, figs.

TRY
All the suggestions for basil (page 136) work equally well for dark opal basil.

DEVELOPED IN THE 1950S at the University of Connecticut, dark opal basil (also called purple basil) is a mottled variety of the green classic. Some say the word 'opal' comes from the Greek *opallios*, for 'alias' or 'alter', hinting at the leaves, which are a luxurious dark purple with a metallic green undertone.

With pale pink flowers and a delicious clove-like, almost minty scent, dark opal basil is grown as much for its ornamental value as for its culinary uses. As the plant matures, its beautiful leaves become even darker purple. The colouring comes from anthocyanins, a substance that is also found in aubergines (eggplant), blood oranges and red perilla leaves (page 155) and is said to contain antioxidants that can protect many of the body's systems.

Dark opal basil can be used in any recipes where you would use green basil. With its warm, spicy flavour and dramatic colour, it makes a particularly good addition to salads and stir-fries. For the most dramatic effect, pair it with white foods, such as risotto, white peaches or soft cheese; try it in a traditional Italian *insalata tricolore* for a twist on the usual patriotic red, green and white colour scheme. If you infuse vinegar with opal basil, the colour will turn the vinegar a delightful shade of mauve. Pesto, too, will be a different shade entirely when made with this variety of basil, and its flavour will have a little extra oomph.

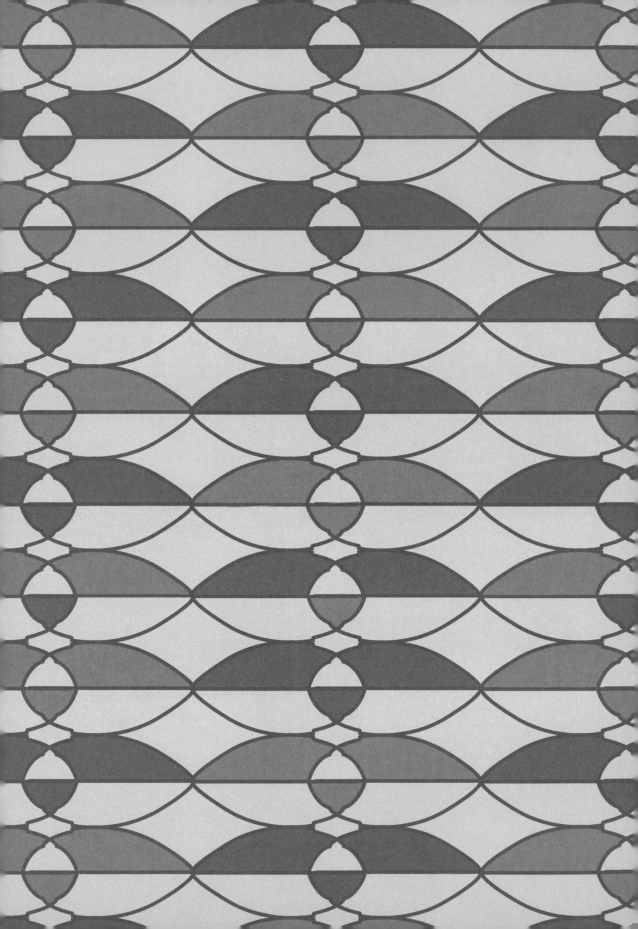

Origanum majorana

Sweet Marjoram

—————

With its unique sweet, flowery scent and suggestion of thyme and citrus, sweet marjoram is an enjoyable and versatile culinary herb.

GROW
Plant in well-drained soil in spring, once the threat of frost has passed. To ensure continued growth, trim the plant when flower buds appear.

EAT WITH
Chicken, lamb, duck, veal, fish, shellfish, chickpeas, carrots, butternut squash, cabbage, spinach, peppers, tomatoes, eggs, garlic, lemons, oranges.

TRY
All the suggestions for oregano (see page 144) work equally well with marjoram.

HEAL
Marjoram tea is said to ease colds and settle upset stomachs, including those unsettled by seasickness.

SWEET MARJORAM GROWS to anywhere between 30 and 100 cm (12–39 in.) tall, its small white flowers forming characteristic 'knots' – hence its alternative name, knotted marjoram. A perennial herb and a member of the Lamiaceae (mint or deadnettle) family, it is a close cousin of oregano, although it adds sweetness and a subtly spicy quality to the oregano mix. The general confusion between the two is explored on page 144. Sweet marjoram was well known in classical times for its medicinal as well as its culinary applications: the ancient Greeks used it as an antidote to poison and to relieve muscle spasms.

The flavour of marjoram is lost if subjected to fierce heat, so always add it towards the end of cooking. Its affinity with meats makes it a popular herb to use in stuffings, where, because it is encased by the meat, it is protected from the heat of the oven. It is one of the best herbs to use in tomato sauces, and also shines in stuffed vegetables, such as peppers and mushrooms.

Origanum vulgare

Oregano

With its warm, slightly sharp taste and hint of camphor, oregano is a herb that communicates its flavour through stewing rather than frying.

GROW
Being a Mediterranean herb, oregano likes well-drained soil and plenty of sunshine. Start it from seed, division or cuttings, beginning indoors and transplanting it outside when the weather gets warmer (above 7°C/45°F).

EAT WITH
Chicken, lamb, duck, veal, fish, shellfish, chickpeas, carrots, butternut squash, cabbage, spinach, peppers, tomatoes, eggs, garlic, lemons, oranges.

TRY
Add oregano to tomato sauce for pizza to give an authentic Italian flavour. Include in stuffings for vegetables such as courgettes, aubergines and peppers. Add to a marinade for kebabs or fish. Give orange or lemon sorbet a twist by infusing the sugar syrup with oregano overnight (this also works well with tomato sorbet).

HEAL
A natural anti-inflammatory and painkiller, oregano is used to treat respiratory tract and gastrointestinal disorders as well as acne and dandruff.

THERE IS MUCH debate about the words used to describe certain herbs. Oregano is one of them, with a dispute among botanists over whether the name refers to a group of plants or a flavour – not to mention its complex relationship with marjoram. It seems to be true to say that all marjorams are oreganos but not all oreganos are marjorams. Marjoram once had its own genus, but now sweet marjoram (see page 143) is only one of over fifty varieties of oregano. To add to the confusion, in North America the name marjoram is often replaced by oregano. There is consolation for the bewildered, though: they are all part of the Lamiaceae (mint or deadnettle) family, easily recognized by their square stems and opposing leaf pairs.

Origanum vulgare has very pretty purple flowers and tiny spade-shaped, olive-green leaves. There are many varieties, from the highly decorative Kent Beauty to the aromatic Greek version. Its name meaning 'joy of the mountain', oregano is such a staple of Greek culture that it is even woven into the crowns worn by bridal couples. It is central to the marinade for souvlaki and many other lamb dishes, and is cooked with vegetables and used in salads. In Italy you will find it on pizzas and in pasta sauces.

With its high thymol content, oregano has always been thought of as a disinfectant and preservative. It was incorporated into nosegays during the sixteenth century in attempts to ward off the plague. In the nineteenth century, herbal doctors prescribed it as a tonic for general wellbeing. A few drops of oregano essential oil on your pillow can aid sleep.

Ginseng

The most prized roots of ginseng are those that are shaped like a person; the Chinese word ginseng *means 'likeness of man'.*

GROW
Simulating ginseng's natural environment is best, and it will take eight years for the ginseng to mature: you'll need to be in a cool, temperate climate with good annual rainfall.

HEAL
Taking ginseng capsules, or infusing ginseng tea bags in boiled water, can help you get some of the energizing potency of ginseng.

A MEMBER OF THE Araliaceae (ivy) family, ginseng is a short, slow-growing perennial plant with fleshy roots that are not ready for use until at least five years old. Supposedly great for boosting the immune system and sex life alike, ginseng has been used by the Chinese as a panacea for 2,000 years, and its Latin name, *Panax* or 'all-healing', reflects that. It was first recommended in AD 100 in the *Shennong Ben Cao Jing* (Classic Herbal of Shennong), a book written by the legendary Chinese ruler Shennong, Emperor of the Five Grains, who allegedly tasted and tested seventy herbs a day.

Ginseng is the remedy of choice for older Chinese people, who think of it as a 'wonder of the world', and in the United States six million people take ginseng regularly. Its active constituents have been shown to strengthen the immune system by stimulating the production of immunoglobin, proteins that bind to foreign substances such as bacteria when they invade the body. It could, potentially, be useful for everything from flu, diabetes and Alzheimer's to impotence and chronic fatigue. Researchers are divided, though, and, as with most herb health claims, it is always best to consult your doctor.

Undisputed, however, is ginseng's status as a worldwide phenomenon. It can be found in everything from herbal tablets to energy drinks to hair tonics; you can even get a *caffè al ginseng* in many Rome cafés. It's a stimulant, of course, so insomnia can be a side effect. One of the weirder international ginseng moments was in 2010, when North Korea offered to make one of its debt repayments to the Czech Republic in ginseng rather than cash.

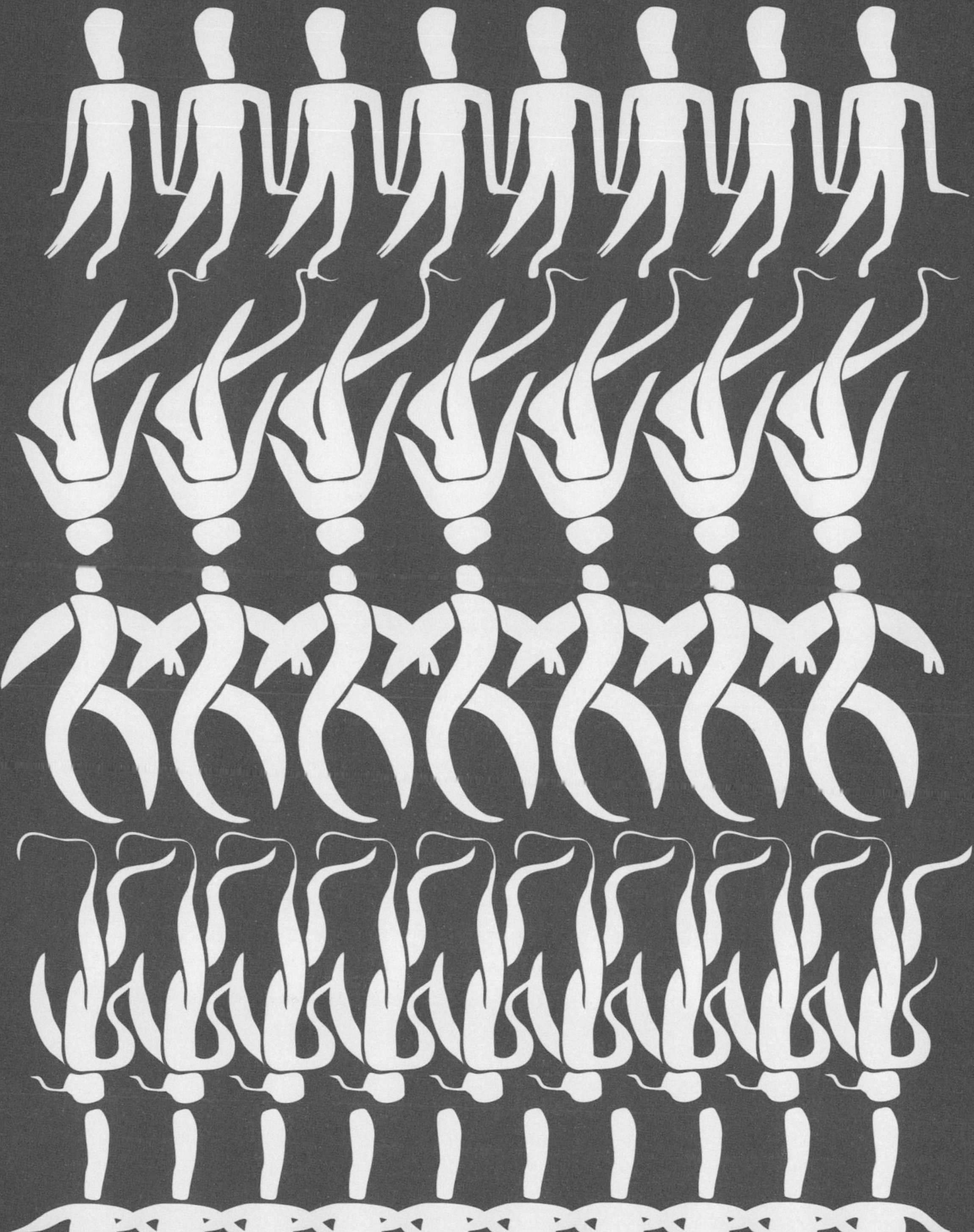

Pandan

———

*A key ingredient in Malaysian and Indonesian cuisine,
pandan leaves, from the screwpine tree, add a distinctive,
slightly nutty aroma to rice and curries.*

GROW
Grow pandan shrubs in full sun. They prefer soil that retains moisture while not getting soggy.

EAT WITH
Chicken, fish, coconut, rice, noodles, cream, lemongrass, ginger, mango, banana.

TRY
Use pieces of pandan leaf to flavour boiled rice, pannacotta or baked custard – it's particularly good in a coconut milk custard.

HEAL
A decoction of the bark can be taken as a tea to help with fever and coughs, or added to bathwater to soothe skin problems.

PANDAN, WHICH IS found throughout Southeast Asia, has shiny, almost sword-like leaves and grows either as a 1-m-high (3 ft) shrub or as a tree of up to 20 m (65 ft) in height. The trees grow easily in damp areas and the leaves can be harvested at any time; the shrubs can be grown in the herb garden, depending, of course, on climate.

Pandan is said to have medicinal benefits, and a decoction of the bark can be taken as a tea or added to the bath to help with skin problems. The leaves are also used in handicrafts: craftsmen collect them from the wild and slice them into fine strips ready for processing. Weavers use the processed strips to make basic mats or ropes, which are then coloured and dried and used as place mats or incorporated into jewellery boxes.

For cooking, the fibrous leaves are used as a flavouring rather than being eaten, typically torn into strips, bruised, tied into knots and placed in the pan to add their lightly musky, mown-grass notes. They can also be used to flavour cakes and creamy desserts, or to wrap chicken, fish, sticky rice or banana leaves into parcels before cooking. For pandan-flavoured sugar, cut the leaves into 2-cm (¾-in.) lengths and place a few pieces in a jar of caster (superfine) sugar.

Poppy

Has my Friend intoxicating eyes
Or has he eyes like ruby-red poppy?

SUFI POEM

GROW
Scatter seeds wherever you have bare soil, and wait for the rain. Poppies can also be grown in pots and planted out. They thrive on plenty of sun.

EAT WITH
Orange, lemon, vanilla, cinnamon, honey, chocolate, dried fruit, nuts, noodles, rice, carrots, potatoes, cabbage, chicken.

TRY
Toast a couple of teaspoons of poppy seeds in a dry frying pan for two to three minutes, until fragrant, then toss them with fresh ribbon pasta such as tagliatelle or fettuccine, plus lemon zest, plenty of butter and some salt and pepper. For a sweet version, substitute icing (confectioners') sugar and vanilla essence for the salt and pepper.

HEAL
A tincture or infusion of red poppy is said to relieve anxiety and stress and act as a mild sedative.

IT WAS THOUGHT that if poppies grew in their fields, farmers would get a bountiful crop – and the poppy (also known as corn rose) has always been associated with Demeter, the goddess of fertility. A single plant can produce an impressive 60,000 seeds – hence the ability to spread like wildfire. Tenacious poppies can lie dormant for as long as fifty years, shining forth only when the ground is disturbed by the plough or, of course, war. Poppies flourished in the battlefields after the First World War, their bright crimson hoods growing up out of the cracks of despair, and they became a symbol of remembrance for the dead, inspiring Lieutenant Colonel John McCrae's famous couplet, 'In Flanders fields the poppies blow/ Between the crosses, row on row.'

An annual herb growing up to 60 cm (2 ft) tall, the poppy has showy scarlet flowers that stand out on long, hairy stalks. The nutty-tasting, slate-grey seeds can be used to flavour sweet and savoury dishes or pressed to make an oil. In Germany and eastern Europe, they make an attractive decoration sprinkled onto breads and cakes; they are also ground and mixed to a paste with sugar, butter and various flavourings as a filling for sweet breads such as the German Mohnstollen and cakes like Mohntorte and the Polish makowiec. Ashkenazi Jews traditionally celebrate Purim with hamantaschen, little triangular poppy-seed pastries. In India, ivory-coloured poppy seeds are ground and used to thicken sauces and curries, or roasted and added to spice mixtures. The young leaves of poppy plants can be eaten raw, before the flower pods have formed, in soups and salads.

Scented Geranium

The great imitators of the herb kingdom, and beloved of the Victorians, scented geraniums come in all kinds, from peach to chocolate peppermint.

GROW
Scented geraniums are much more reliably propagated by cuttings than from seed. After the initial watering, keep cuttings as dry as possible to avoid blackleg disease.

TRY
Make subtly scented cakes by lining the bottom of the cake tin with geranium leaves, removing them when the cake has cooled.

HEAL
A cup of rose-scented geranium tea strengthens the endocrine system and reduces stress. Geranium is also believed to have anti-inflammatory qualities, which is good for sore joints and aching muscles.

AND IT'S THE scented leaves, funnily enough, not the beautiful flowers, that do all the hard work of flavour and aroma. There are hundreds of scented geraniums, smelling of everything from apple and clove through to rose and mint. There's *Pelargonium capitatum*, also known as *P.* 'Attar of Roses', which is used commercially for its essential oil. Geranium sugar can be made with it by putting several leaves into a jar of sugar for a few weeks; use the sugar in desserts and cakes to scent your food with rose. Or go orange, with *P. citrosum*, American Prince of Orange, for a strong citrus scent. Make a mint-flavoured tisane with *P. tomentosum*, also known as *P.* 'Chocolate Peppermint', whose leaves have dark-brown blotches across the centre. If you are growing this one, make sure you give it enough bright light or it will stay green. There are plenty more varieties, but do look out for *P.* 'Ardwick Cinnamon', to give a warmly spicy flavour and scent to cakes, biscuits and cookies, and *P. graveolens* (rose geranium), for that hit of Turkish delight.

Scented geraniums were discovered at the Cape of Good Hope in the 1620s by John Tradescant, the English king Charles I's chief botanist. The Victorians went crazy for them in England and grew them in heated greenhouses until 1914, when the practice was stopped in order to conserve energy for the war effort.

Perilla

———

Also known by its Japanese name, shiso, *perilla – whose seeds are rich in omega-3 fatty acids – is a Chinese herb related to basil and mint.*

GROW
Perilla likes partial shade. Grow it as you would any annual herb, starting it off indoors in spring, or sowing it outside in early summer.

EAT WITH
Beef, chicken, fish, potatoes, rice, noodles, tomatoes.

TRY
Substitute perilla for basil to make an Asian-inspired pesto. Toss chopped green perilla into noodle and rice dishes or use to garnish fish stews. Use the leaves whole to wrap meat or fish before cooking.

HEAL
In modern Chinese medicine, a decoction or infusion of perilla is used for common colds, stuffy noses, coughs and headaches, for dispersing stagnant *qi* and calming the mind.

IT HAS A sweet scent and surprising notes of cumin, anise and cinnamon, as well as cool, minty undertones. The spade-like leaves of green perilla stand out in a crowd. They're exciting to look at, with jagged, crinkly edges, reminiscent of stinging nettles. Green perilla is often used in Japanese cooking – most familiarly in sushi and sashimi, but also in soups and salads.

Rich in vitamins A, C and K and high in calcium, perilla also comes in a red variety, whose leaves range from deep red to burgundy-bronze. They are more finely serrated than those of green perilla and look beautiful in salads, bringing an interesting colour contrast. Subtler in flavour and aroma than the green ones, these gorgeous red leaves are often used as a garnish for sashimi in Japan and can be turned into a sweet-sharp drink made with sugar, vinegar and lemon juice.

Persicaria odorata

Rau Răm

A very popular herb in Southeast Asian cooking, rau răm is also known as Vietnamese mint (or Vietnamese coriander) or laksa leaf, and by its Malay name, daun kesom.

GROW
It is possible to grow rau răm in a container using a loam-based potting compost (soil mix), but keep it out of the midday sun. Water regularly from spring to autumn, and protect from frost.

EAT WITH
Seafood, fish, chicken, pork, noodles, peanuts, lettuce, carrots, garlic, green papaya, ginger.

TRY
Use whole rau răm leaves in Vietnamese summer rolls, along with beansprouts, shredded carrot, cooked prawns (shrimp), rice noodles, lemongrass and mint, rolled up in rice paper wrappers and served with a dipping sauce.

HEAL
An infusion of rau răm leaves has been used since ancient times for its soothing properties. The herb is said to help with poor digestion, flatulence and inappropriate or excessive sexual urges. The Australian chef Christine Manfield recommends laksa – that fiery noodle soup – for 'deep slurp therapy'.

RAU RĂM, WHICH looks very much like mint, is indigenous throughout the tropics and subtropics of southern and eastern Asia, where it is used in both food and medicine. It is a common treatment for indigestion, flatulence and stomach ache, and even unwanted sexual desire. There is a Vietnamese saying, '*Rau răm, giá sống*', meaning, 'Rau răm, raw beansprouts'. It refers to the fact that the former is thought to suppress sexual urges while the latter have the opposite effect. There are no scientific studies to back this up, but Buddhist monks are said to grow rau răm in their herb gardens to help them lead celibate lives.

The leaves have a mild taste at first, with a hint of lime and spice, but become more peppery and fiery. They are great torn over stir-fries and phos (noodle soups), and work as a substitute for coriander (cilantro) in most dishes. It is with Vietnamese cooking that rau răm is particularly associated: in salads, soups, stews and fresh spring rolls, also known as summer rolls, which are made with translucent rice wrappers. Rau răm is also a staple ingredient in the laksas of Malaysia and Singapore, hence its alternative name laksa leaf.

Petroselinum crispum var. *neapolitanum*

Parsley

Isabella Mary (Mrs) Beeton, the author of the much reprinted
Book of Household Management *(1861), pronounces*
'this beautiful herb the emblem of joy and festivity'.

GROW
Given parsley's
Mediterranean origins, it
grows best – usually from
seed – in moist, well-drained
soil in full sun.

EAT WITH
Parsley goes with pretty
much every savoury
ingredient imaginable.

TRY
Make a salsa verde: very
finely chop two garlic cloves,
2 tablespoons capers, six
anchovies, two large handfuls
of flat-leaf parsley and a small
bunch each of basil and mint.
Mix with 1 tablespoon Dijon
mustard and 3 tablespoons
red wine vinegar, then slowly
stir in enough extra-virgin
olive oil to make a thick
sauce. Season, then taste
and tweak the flavour to your
liking. (You can make this
in a food processor, too, but
be careful not to process it
to a paste.)

HEAL
Whizz a bunch of parsley into
any juice. Parsley tea, made
by infusing a bunch in boiling
water for twenty minutes, is
a good source of iron and can
help to clear the complexion.

TO BE CLEAR, we are talking about the flat-leaf cultivar here, although curly parsley (*Petroselinum crispum*), which is slightly more bitter and textured, has its own merits.

Flat-leaf parsley is the most versatile, possibly the most useful and certainly one of the most graceful herbs in the kitchen, with its wonderful lightness of touch and its clean, green flavour, which evokes the mown lawns of spring. It is rich in vitamins, including A, B12, C and K, as well as a number of essential flavonoid components with seeming antioxidant effects.

A native of the central Mediterranean, parsley is, of course, not without its history and mythology. The ancient Greeks esteemed it so highly that they crowned victors at the Isthmian Games with it. It is said that if you have a grudge against someone, you can simply pick up some parsley and utter their name, and they will be dead within days.

Parsley's role in the kitchen is well known, although all too often it is relegated to the status of garnish rather than being used as a flavour in its own right. Dishes in which it is given due prominence include salsa verde, tabbouleh, gremolata and chimichurri. The French *jambon persillé* is a terrine of diced ham held together by a parsley-flecked meat jelly. In British cooking, parsley sauce, made by adding chopped parsley to a béchamel sauce, is a classic accompaniment to fish or ham.

Portulaca oleracea

Purslane

———

*Also known as fatweed, pussly and verdolaga, purslane
is a fatter, more succulent version of lamb's lettuce (corn
salad), with a refreshing, lemony taste.*

GROW
Simply scatter the seeds over
the ground. There is no need
to cover them with soil, since
they need light to germinate.

EAT WITH
Beetroot, cucumber,
tomatoes, peppers, red
onions, spinach, beans,
feta cheese, goat's cheese,
yogurt, chilli, olives, nuts.

TRY
Combine sprigs of young
purslane with diced
watermelon, chunks of feta
cheese and a light vinaigrette
to make a cooling salad for
a hot day.

HEAL
Graze on purslane, add it to
juices and chop it through
mixed salads to get all the
benefits of its very high
levels of omega-3 fatty
acids, which can promote a
healthier cholesterol balance
in the bloodstream.

COMPARISONS ABOUND: PURSLANE is also like watercress –
though milder and crunchier – and it can be substituted for spinach.
And a quick note here: we're talking about what is also known as
summer purslane; the name winter purslane is reserved for miner's
lettuce, or *Claytonia perfoliata* (see page 64).

Purslane's high omega-3 fatty acid content is in its favour,
gaining it comparisons with fish, algae and flax seeds. It is also very
high in vitamins A, B and C and magnesium and calcium, which can
boost the immune system, reduce headaches and support a healthy
heart. The herb was even recommended as an agreeable addition
to salads in John Evelyn's *Discourse of Sallets* (1699), possibly the
first ever diet cookbook. In Evelyn's time, purslane was purported
to be beneficial for anyone suffering from arthritis, heart disease or
toothache.

Purslane is certainly an international leaf, having distributed
itself throughout Europe, North Africa, the Middle East, the Indian
subcontinent and Australasia. In Greece – where the herb is called
glistrida (slippery), supposedly because it turns the eater into a
chatterbox – it is often paired with onions, garlic and thick yogurt
or used in the classic Greek village salad with feta and cucumber.
It is a standard component of the Lebanese salad fattoush, while
in Turkey it is cooked as a vegetable or added to baked pastries,
and in Pakistan it is included in lentil stews.

Cowslip

'Where the bee sucks, there suck I; in a cowslip's bell I lie.'

WILLIAM SHAKESPEARE, THE TEMPEST

GROW
Cowslips prefer a sunny spot in a garden with neutral to slightly alkaline soil. They can also be grown in containers and look great in window boxes.

TRY
Add young cowslip leaves and flowers to salads. Include the leaves in meat stuffings. Make a cowslip tisane by steeping 2 teaspoons of cowslip petals in boiled water for ten to fifteen minutes.

HEAL
A sedative cowslip tea made from the leaves or flowers can treat insomnia. A cowslip syrup – made with crushed flowers, honey and water – can also help with coughs and asthma. Herbalists use cowslip in skin cleansers to treat acne and blemishes. Do note, though, that cowslips can cause contact dermatitis.

THE COMMON NAME of this true spring flower (its Latin name means 'the first little one of spring'), chiefly found in clay soil, comes from the Old English *cuslyppe*, meaning 'cow dung'. Perhaps the scalloped leaves in the rosettes look like cowpats from afar, or maybe it is simply because the cowslip often grows in cow pastures. Strangely enough, this much-loved herb has also been compared to a bunch of keys: it is said that St Peter dropped his, and cowslips grew where they landed. This would certainly explain the cowslip's other common name: keys of heaven.

If foraging, remember that it is illegal in many countries to uproot the cowslip (or any other wild flower); just pick leaves and flowers as required. It might be best to grow your own, as the cowslip has been declining for decades in some countries as a result of agricultural farming, herbicides and chemical fertilizers.

Cowslips have been used medicinally for all sorts of ailment. The sixteenth-century herbalist John Gerard said: 'A conserve made with the flowers. . .prevaileth woonderfully against the palsie.' For years, cowslip leaves have been used to make a sedative tea to treat insomnia, and the roots to treat whooping cough.

This traditional herb is edible both fresh and dried, as flowers, roots or leaves. The flowers and leaves, which have a delicate, sweet taste, are rich in beta-carotene and vitamin C and can lower cholesterol levels. Cowslip wine is made from the 'peeps' – the yellow petal rings – mixed with sugar, lemon, spring water and fresh yeast.

Primrose

A primrose by a river's brim
A yellow primrose was to him,
And it was nothing more.
WILLIAM WORDSWORTH, 'PETER BELL', 1798

GROW
Sow seeds in July or August and transplant seedlings in autumn, when they are well grown.

TRY
Scatter primrose flowers over salads or use them to decorate cakes and desserts.

HEAL
A primrose tisane can act as a mild sedative; a decoction of the roots can alleviate bronchial problems and coughs.

PRIMROSES THRIVE IN damp, shady areas and are a perennial plant, heralding the start of spring. Common in Britain, continental Europe and North America, they grow in lightly wooded areas, near hedges and along forest edges. Bees love them. In the United Kingdom and many other countries it is illegal to dig up or pick these once-endangered flowers, so they are worth growing yourself.

The primrose has fibrous roots and a rosette of leaves with undulating margins. The flower stalk bears five to twelve funnel-shaped flowers during April and May, followed by a cluster of pods filled with many seeds. There are two kinds of flower: pin-eyed and thrum-eyed. In the centre of the pin-eyed flower is the green knob of the stigma, like a pin's head; the thrum-eyed has its stigma further down the tube. It was Charles Darwin who spotted something interesting about this: it means that when a long-tongued insect visits a thrum-eyed flower after a pin-eyed one (or vice versa), the pollen is on the right part of its proboscis to rub onto the stigma, thus promoting cross-pollination. The rest is, as they say, evolution.

Primroses were loved by famous herbalists of yore. Pliny talked of the primrose as an important remedy for muscular rheumatism, paralysis and gout. Nicholas Culpeper said: 'Of the leaves of Primrose is made as fine a salve to heal wounds as any I know.' And John Gerard recommended that primrose tea be 'drunk in the month of May' for 'curing the phrensie'. The early twentieth-century herbalist Mrs Grieve wrote about an old recipe for primrose pottage – a thick soup or stew made using the flowers – as well as a pilaf with rice, almonds, honey, saffron and ground primroses.

Rorippa nasturtium-aquaticum

Watercress

With little by way of aroma and much by way of peppery green vibrancy, watercress – once eaten by Roman emperors to help them make 'bold decisions' – is the ultimate 'superfood'.

GROW

To prosper, watercress must be kept continuously wet. It can grow either in water or in damp soil, if the water is kept fresh. Sow on the surface of the soil; it does not need covering with extra compost (soil mix).

EAT WITH

Chicken, beef, duck, fish, carrots, cucumber, onions, fennel, potatoes, peas, cheese, oranges, pears, nuts, eggs, sorrel.

TRY

If you have a juice extractor, make a gloriously green, nutrient-packed drink by juicing a bunch of watercress with two apples and two celery stalks or a cucumber, adding a little lemon juice if you like.

HEAL

With its potential to reduce the risk of various cancers and cardiovascular diseases, improve bone health and help the body maintain healthy levels of calcium, the best advice is to practise watercress versatility: graze from the bag, make juices, add to soups at the end of cooking, use in sandwiches, make pesto. . .

AND RIGHTLY SO: watercress contains more calcium than milk, more iron than spinach and more vitamin C than oranges. Indeed, this tangy leaf is packed with at least fifteen essential vitamins and minerals. It is no wonder, then, that Hippocrates, the father of medicine, positioned his first hospital next to a stream. This meant that he could grow a plentiful supply of watercress.

The best way to take advantage of all that nutritional goodness is to eat watercress raw. Bracing and refreshing, it is a good counterpoint to rich foods, such as duck, smoked fish and creamy sauces. Counteract Christmas excess with a salad of watercress and orange. The mustardy flavour softens when it is cooked, and so it makes one of the most pleasing soups. Potato and watercress soup is a classic in many countries – in France it used to be known as *potage de santé*, or health soup – while in Italy watercress is sometimes added to minestrone. In China, the leaves are blanched briefly and tossed in sesame oil. Don't forget the joys of the watercress sandwich, using the leaves either on their own or with chicken, turkey, beef or cheese. If making a salad, add the flowers and leaves of watercress's cousin, the nasturtium (*Tropaeolum*), for a cress-like flavour.

Perhaps unsurprisingly, given that there's so much to celebrate about this hardy native European perennial, there is an annual Watercress Festival in the English town of Alresford and a railway line called the Watercress Line. A warning for foragers: do not pick watercress downstream of grazing cattle or sheep because of the risk of the parasite liver fluke.

Rose

'Rose is a rose is a rose is a rose.'
GERTRUDE STEIN, 'SACRED EMILY', 1913

GROW
Plant roses in the garden or in containers, watering well in dry spells for at least two summers after planting.

EAT WITH
Strawberries, apricots, peaches, raspberries, apples, cucumber, vanilla, honey, saffron, almonds, cinnamon, lemon, orange, lamb, quail.

TRY
Add a little rosewater to buttercream to decorate a cake or cupcakes (use sparingly, or your cake will be too perfumed), then scatter fresh, unsprayed rose petals over the top. Make a rose Bellini: infuse sugar syrup with rose petals, bolstering the flavour with rosewater if necessary, then strain and add a teaspoonful to a glass of Champagne or Prosecco.

HEAL
Rose essential oil can lift the mind; rosehips can reduce blood pressure; rosewater can be used in skincare preparations; and rose tea is calming and anti-inflammatory, traditionally used for menstrual complaints.

IT MIGHT BE peculiar to think of a rose as a herb, but this outstanding plant with its glorious flowers has for centuries been as useful as it is beautiful. Of course, there are many different kinds of rose, with about 3,000 varieties available to grow. Herbalists tend to use classic roses rather than hybrids, and never those that have been sprayed with chemicals. Medicinally, the plant's goodness is in the petals. They contain compounds that can improve the metabolism, as well as antioxidants and antibacterial compounds to soothe the skin and treat acne when splashed on as rosewater. This can also be added to natural beauty and skincare formulations or used in baths. Rose tincture has been cherished for centuries as a treatment for sadness, grief, depression and insomnia.

Rosehips can be gathered from hedgerows in England. They are surprisingly useful in the kitchen, in syrup, cordial, jelly, vinegar and even chutney. Given their whopping 2000 mg of vitamin C per 100 g, these are healthy options. Rose petals are a delight to use in cooking, either dried or in the form of rosewater. In India, North Africa and the Middle East, rosewater appears not just in sweet dishes such as the Indian kheer and kulfi, and drinks such as lassi, but also in savoury biryanis and lamb stews, where rose is often combined with gentle spices such as saffron, cinnamon and cardamom. In Morocco rosewater is added to a carrot salad with coriander and cumin. Perhaps the rose's most famous culinary use is in Turkish delight, but it also crops up in baklava in Turkey. Dried rose petals are added to the Moroccan spice mix ras-el-hanout, while fresh ones can be added to desserts or made into a delicate, floral jam.

Rosmarinus officinalis

Rosemary

Possibly the most poignant use of a herb in the history of literature occurs in Shakespeare's Hamlet*: Ophelia, turned mad through grief, measures out her sadness – 'There's rosemary, that's for remembrance.'*

GROW

Rosemary is easy to grow, particularly if it is propagated from cuttings. Plant in a sunny spot and prune regularly to prevent it from getting lanky. Water evenly.

EAT WITH

Lamb, beef, pork, veal, rabbit, chicken, peppers, tomatoes, onions, potatoes, cabbage, parsnips, squash, oily fish, lentils, anchovies, olives, chocolate, apples, pears, plums, oranges.

TRY

If you have a mature rosemary bush in your garden, strip the leaves from a few stout branches and use the stalks as skewers for seafood or chicken kebabs, sharpening the ends first.

HEAL

An infusion of rosemary can be taken for tiredness and headaches; a massage rub can soothe aching joints; inhaling essential oil from a tissue can stimulate the brain. Researchers are looking into the use of rosemary to enhance memory performance.

AND ROSEMARY – literally, 'dew of the sea' – has always been thrown into graves to signify remembrance, just as brides have for a long time worn rosemary headpieces (they are thought to be a love charm). Love and death go hand in hand when it comes to this woody, evergreen perennial, as the seventeenth-century poet Robert Herrick knew: 'Grow for two ends – it matters not at all, Be't for my bridall, or my buriall.'

This powerfully aromatic herb, native to the Mediterranean, has lovely blue, butterfly-attracting flowers and blue-grey foliage. Despite its origin, though, it flourishes in cooler climates and is a staple in British gardens. In culinary terms, rosemary is best used with a certain amount of discretion, since this resinous, slightly bitter-tasting herb, with its notes of camphor and nutmeg, can be strong. It is a natural accompaniment to roast meat – so much so that, in Italy and France, butchers are in the habit of giving customers a small bunch to cook with their purchase. The partnership with lamb is perhaps best known – tiny sprigs of rosemary, slivers of garlic and sometimes anchovy are inserted into slits in a leg of lamb before roasting – but it works well in most robust savoury dishes and is particularly good scattered over sautéed potatoes or roast squash towards the end of cooking. It also makes a surprisingly successful addition to desserts; poach a sprig or two with autumn fruits, add it to an apple pie or use it to flavour a dark chocolate ganache or mousse. Rosemary flowers can be frozen in ice cubes to make a pretty addition to summer cocktails.

Sorrel

———

A great accompaniment to white fish, or in a soup with haricot beans, sorrel is – as the sound of its name implies – a sour one.

GROW

Sorrel likes well-drained soil in full sun. Bear in mind that because it self-seeds, it can get out of control and be difficult to eradicate. It makes an excellent container plant, however.

EAT WITH

Chicken, pork, fish, eggs, leeks, potatoes, cucumber, lentils, lettuce, beans, tomatoes, watercress.

TRY

Make a sorrel sauce: roll up a bunch of sorrel leaves and slice them thinly, then cook gently in butter until they collapse. Add thick cream to cover, bring to a simmer and season to taste. Serve with fish: it is particularly good with salmon fishcakes.

HEAL

Eat sorrel in moderate amounts (its levels of oxalic acid call for some restraint) to improve eyesight, strengthen the immune system, improve digestion and build strong bones.

THE FOOD WRITER, television presenter and 'real food' campaigner Hugh Fearnley-Whittingstall admits that sorrel is 'one of my favourite leaves to eat and cook with in spring and early summer'. This member of the dock family is not often spotted in shops and markets, partly because it wilts quickly, so it is a great herb to grow at home. Tangy and lemony in flavour, with a secret sharpness thanks to oxalic acid, sorrel has a texture similar to spinach.

The good news is that it is simple to grow. Sorrel is self-seeding, so it just gets on with it (rather too well, some might say). If you cut off the flower spikes before they open, it will stay productive.

Or, of course, you could go foraging. Sorrel grows wild in damp pastures and fertile places. It tends to flower quickly, after which the leaves shrink and toughen, so you can forage for it only in spring. There's also sheep sorrel, with tiny leaves that are more than pleasurable to graze on while you do some idle cloud-spotting. Sorrel could help with all kinds of spotting, in fact: some studies indicate that this vitamin A-rich herb could lower the risk of cataracts.

Sorrel's astringency makes it an obvious choice for perking up gentle foods such as eggs, cream, rice, potatoes and fish. Be aware, though, that heat causes it to lose its colour and collapse into a grey-green sludge – delicious to eat, less so to look at.

Salvia officinalis

Sage

*English folklore has it that sage grows best in households
where the wife is dominant.*

GROW
Sage likes warm, well-drained soil and sun. The leaves can be harvested from spring to autumn; cut the plants back after flowering.

EAT WITH
Pork, bacon, chicken, turkey, goose, duck, offal, onions, potatoes, squash, green beans, apples, polenta, blue cheese.

TRY
Make sage and anchovy fritters to serve with drinks: sandwich an anchovy fillet between two large sage leaves, dip in flour, then in lightly beaten egg, then in breadcrumbs. Deep-fry in hot oil until crisp and golden.

HEAL
An infusion of sage leaves can help digestion and menopausal symptoms. Gargle the infusion for sore throats and tonsillitis, or use it as a hair rinse for dandruff.

IN FACT, IT grows best in warm, dry soil, being a native of the northern Mediterranean. The name derives from the Latin *salvus*, meaning healthy. Sage was used to keep teeth clean and relieve sore gums, while an infusion was said to alleviate arthritis. Nowadays it is the herb you reach for when you need that certain musky quality and warmly spiced, balsamic taste.

Sage is still associated with aiding digestion, since it is so often paired with fatty foods, such as pork, duck and goose. In Britain its use is pretty much restricted to a stuffing with onions and apples for poultry or pork, or as a seasoning for sausages. Sage Derby cheese, which uses the herb for colour and flavour, fell out of favour for a while, although some cheesemakers are now reviving it. The Italians sizzle sage briefly in melted butter to pour over stuffed pasta or meat; combine it with blue cheese as a sauce for pasta or polenta; and encase it in Parma ham with veal or pork escalopes to make saltimbocca. The leaves can also be deep-fried to make a crisp garnish that is particularly good with liver.

The cookery and travel writer Patience Gray wrote fondly of a recipe for *aigo bouido*, 'boiled water', an ancient remedy made with sage. This Provençal lifesaver – helpful for physical debility, hangover and liver complaints – is made from slightly salted water, two crushed garlic cloves, two sprigs of sage and a spoonful of olive oil. 'Boiled for 15 minutes, this infusion is strained and poured slowly into a plate in which a fresh egg yolk is sitting'; stirring the yolk naturally thickens the water.

Elder

*'Grow patience! And let the stinking elder, grief, untwine his
perishing root with the increasing vine!'*
WILLIAM SHAKESPEARE, CYMBELINE

GROW
If elder doesn't grow readily
in your area, you could
cultivate your own elder tree
by sowing ripe berries in a
pot outdoors and leaving it
in a sunny spot. If foraging,
pick on a dry, sunny day to
maximize sweetness.

EAT WITH
Elderflowers: gooseberries,
rhubarb, apples, strawberries,
raspberries, lemon.
Elderberries: apples, pears,
plums, game, pork.

TRY
Stir elderflowers into a plain
cake mixture, then decorate
the finished cake with an
icing made of elderflower
cordial mixed with sugar and
lemon juice, scattering a few
flowers on top before the
icing sets. Add a couple of
handfuls of elderberries to
a fruit crumble (crisp), a pie
or an upside-down cake.

HEAL
Gargle an infusion of the
flowers for mouth ulcers,
sore throats and tonsillitis;
a syrup made from a
decoction of the berries
mixed with honey can
soothe colds and flu.

AS WELL AS WITH GRIEF, elder has many religious, spiritual and
magical associations: Judas was hanged from an elder tree; the Holy
Cross on which Christ was crucified was made from elder; while in
Denmark, the dryad Hylde-Moer, the elder-tree mother, lived in
elder trees, watching over them and haunting anyone who chopped
them down. In Russia, elder trees were thought to drive away evil
spirits; in Serbia, elder brought good luck to wedding ceremonies;
and in England, the elder was believed never to be struck by
lightning, while an elder twig tied into three knots and carried
in the pocket was used as a charm against rheumatism.

The flowers and berries should be eaten cooked, since they
are mildly toxic when raw. The delicate, lacy flower heads are most
famously used to make elderflower cordial, but they are also good
dipped in a light batter, deep-fried and served sprinkled with sugar.
It is customary to add a sprig or two of elderflower to gooseberries
during cooking – one of those sensational combinations that result
from two ingredients fortuitously being in season at the same time.

The berries are used in syrups, jellies, jams and chutneys, and
also to make wine or vinegar. In puddings, their dominant flavour
is best softened by the inclusion of other fruit, such as apples,
blackberries, pears or plums. A handful of berries thrown into the
roasting tin of a game bird when making gravy gives a deep colour
and autumnal flavour. Use elder plants with care; each species has
different poisonous parts. Always check before you pick.

Salad Burnet

With its toothed, fern-like leaves, salad burnet – also known as drumsticks – is a fine dark green perennial.

GROW
Grow from seed in a spot that gets plenty of sun. Removing the pink and purple flower heads and cutting the leaves regularly will encourage new growth, as will dividing the plant in the second year.

EAT WITH
Soft cheese, fish, eggs, broad (fava) beans, cucumber, tomatoes, mushrooms.

TRY
Stir a handful of salad burnet into a mushroom soup. Toss chopped salad burnet with broad beans and butter. Scatter the herb generously over grilled or fried fish. Mix with cream cheese or with tuna and mayonnaise for a sandwich filling.

HEAL
Both the leaves and the roots are said to soothe digestive complaints, and burnet leaves are said to have anti-inflammatory properties.

SALAD BURNET WAS used by medieval herbalists to stop internal and external bleeding and to heal wounds (the Latin *sanguisorba* means 'soaks up blood'). The sixteenth-century Flemish herbalist Rembert Dodoens said of salad burnet: 'The leaves stiped in wine and drunken doth comfort and rejoice the heart.' Nowadays, alas, we talk in different (less poetic) terms, but to similar effect: salad burnet roots, leaves and stems are thought to contain glycosides, which can lower cholesterol, improve bone health and stimulate the immune system.

With a slightly nutty, cucumber-cum-melon flavour, salad burnet makes a pleasantly mild addition to salads, particularly autumnal ones. The Italians even have a proverb for it: 'Salad is neither good nor pretty without burnet.' It is often used in combination with other herbs – for example, in butters, soups and fish dishes. It also makes an intriguing replacement for tarragon or chives and combines well with them in a *fines herbes* mix. The flowers can be used to garnish salads or decorate cakes.

In the sixteenth century salad burnet leaves were floated as a garnish in goblets of wine. Crushed and added to a gin and tonic or Pimm's, the leaves and flowers give a fresh, herbal kick. Add them to a large pitcher of iced water with lemon for a refreshing soft drink.

Cotton Lavender

An aromatic, dwarf evergreen with button-like yellow or white flower heads, cotton lavender is a native of southern France and the northern Mediterranean, traditionally used in knot gardens.

GROW
Grow from seed or cuttings in moist but well-drained soil in a sunny spot. Trim back after flowering to keep a dense shrub.

THE FORMAL 'CURIOUS-KNOTTED garden' (as mentioned in Shakespeare's *Love's Labour's Lost*) was first established in the reign of Queen Elizabeth I, having possibly been brought to England by French Huguenot gardeners. Designed in a square frame, knot gardens were often made as puzzles to be solved or as symbols of love, featuring aromatic and culinary herbs such as marjoram (page 143), thyme (page 199), lemon balm (page 116), camomile (page 59) and cotton lavender. They feature a continuous hedge of compact evergreens, the spaces between either filled with bronze gravel – for a kind of child-sized maze – or planted with beautiful flowers. The use of evergreens makes knot gardens arresting from inside the house, even in winter. They are best seen from above; John Speed's plans for Henry VIII's now non-existent Nonsuch Palace in Surrey show that the knot gardens were designed specially to be viewed from upper-floor windows.

Cotton lavender – which is not related to either cotton or lavender – is a dense, silver-leaved, aromatic plant with a camomile-like aroma. As well as featuring in knot gardens, the foliage was dried and added to herbal tobacco blends and potpourri. It also makes a good moth deterrent if left in drawers and under carpets or added to a herbal moth bag along with equal parts of dried mint, lavender, sage and rosemary. In medieval times, the herb was applied to wounds to encourage scars to form. Nicholas Culpeper tells us that it was used to 'resist poison, putrefaction and heal the biting of venomous beasts'. Nowadays, though, it is rarely used for medicinal purposes.

Sassafras

———

*Sassafras trees grow anything up to 35 m (115 ft) tall, with
slender branches, smooth, orange-brown bark and fragrant,
yellow-green flowers.*

HEAL
Sassafras tea may aid
digestion and purify the
blood. Fresh sassafras
contains safrole, a known
carcinogen, so be sure
to find a safrole-free
sassafras tea.

AN AROMATIC ORNAMENTAL tree native to eastern North
America, sassafras is commonly found in open woods and along
fences or in fields. It grows well in moist soil, and its dispersal is
mostly down to birds swallowing its seeds when eating the attractive
berries. In fact, the sassafras tree is much loved by many animals,
which like to chew on the bark.

In Louisiana, the leaves are used for their spicy citrus flavour
and to thicken sauces. Ground sassafras leaves, known as filé powder,
are a distinctive feature of Creole and Cajun cuisine. Filé powder
is the key constituent of gumbo, a substantial, spicy soup made
with vegetables, rice and seafood or meat. The powder tastes slightly
sour, with notes of wood and lemon sorrel, and its flavour is brought
out by heating. Root beer was traditionally made from sassafras
roots or bark.

Native Americans used sassafras leaves to treat wounds by
rubbing the leaves directly into them, and indeed, modern research
has shown that sassafras bark has analgesic and antiseptic properties.
It has been used by medicinal herbalists to treat rheumatism
and skin eruptions and as a disinfectant, although some dispute
surrounds this.

Summer Savory

Often associated with beans – its German name,
Bohnenkraut, *means 'bean herb' – summer savory is a*
native of southern Europe and North Africa, particularly
around the Mediterranean.

GROW
Plant the seeds in late spring, preferably in slightly alkaline soil, and harvest the leaves when the flower buds begin to show.

EAT WITH
Lamb, pork, chicken, turkey, game, fish, eggs, onions, potatoes, tomatoes, green beans.

TRY
Add finely chopped summer savory to lentil or raw carrot salads. Make a simple marinade for grilled chicken by mixing plenty of chopped summer savory with olive oil and lemon juice.

HEAL
Savory has been used to help with sleepiness, tinnitus, indigestion and bee and wasp stings. It also has a reputation as an aphrodisiac; indeed, it was a staple ingredient in the love potions of the ancient Egyptians.

SUMMER SAVORY IS highly aromatic and has been used in food preparation for over 2,000 years. The flavour is intense and peppery, so be sparing with it. Its close relation, winter savory – known as *poivre d'âne,* or donkey pepper, in France – has a more piney, sage-like taste. Summer savory is frequently used with beans (which is hardly surprising, since it is known to prevent flatulence), and works well with all kinds, from chickpeas and lentils to fresh borlotti and green beans. It is also good with meats, particularly when included in sausages or stuffings. A tomato sauce is enhanced by a sprig or two of summer savory. The French are particularly fond of this herb, and it forms part of their dried herb mix *herbes de Provence.*

Goldenrod

———

Goldenrod is a healing herb; its genus name, Solidago,
comes from the Latin for 'to make whole'.

GROW
Sow seeds in fertile, moist,
well-drained soil with plenty
of sun and some light
shade. It is possible to grow
goldenrod in pots, but they
will improve a border if you
have one.

HEAL
Goldenrod is sometimes
recommended for colds and
flu, allergies, kidney stones,
arthritis and gout. It is taken
as a tea made from the dried
herb, as capsules or as liquid
extract.

ORIGINALLY IMPORTED FROM the Middle East, goldenrod is
now common in Europe and the Americas, where it flourishes on
waste ground and on roadsides. It grows anything up to 1 m (3 ft)
tall (it can also crawl horizontally), with bright gold-yellow, daisy-like
flower heads. Although popular in herbaceous (perennial) borders
in the early twentieth century, it subsequently went out of fashion,
but it has attained new popularity in the twenty-first century with
the rise of the prairie planting style. The larger goldenrods, such
as *Solidago gigantea* and *S. canadensis*, are worth introducing into the
wilder parts of your garden; they can be invasive, but the butterflies
will have a field day.

Folklore recommends goldenrod for people who are grieving.
Medicinally, it has been used to heal wounds, as a diuretic and to
treat tuberculosis, diabetes, asthma and arthritis. Recent studies tend
to support its diuretic properties, and it is used to help with kidney
stones and treat inflammatory diseases of the urinary tract.

The flowers and leaves can be dried for making potpourri
and tisanes. A more surprising use is for tyres: in the 1920s Henry
Ford gave Thomas Edison a Model T Ford with tyres made from
goldenrod, which contains rubber.

Stevia

This leafy plant from the sunflower family is also known as sweetleaf.

A TENDER PERENNIAL NATIVE to parts of Brazil and Paraguay, stevia favours humid, wet environments and is known for its super-sweet leaves. It is the source of an extracted compound, stevioside, a natural, non-calorific sweetener that can be added to drinks or food.

The Guarani people of Brazil and Paraguay called stevia *ka'a he'ê* – literally, 'sweet herb' – and used it to sweeten the local *yerba maté* tea, as a medicine, and simply to chew. It was 'discovered' (it had been used by indigenous people since ancient times) in 1887 by the Italian botanist Moisés Santiago Bertoni. He wrote: 'In placing in the mouth the smallest particle of any portion of the leaf or twig, one is surprised at the strange and extreme sweetness contained therein. A fragment of the leaf only a few square millimetres in size suffices to keep the mouth sweet for an hour; a few small leaves are sufficient to sweeten a strong cup of coffee or tea.' He named the plant in honour of the Paraguayan chemist Ovidio Rebaudi.

Stevia leaves are said to be highly nutritious, containing beta-carotene, antioxidants and minerals. Good-quality leaves are 300 times sweeter than sugar but with a glycaemic index of zero, meaning that stevia does not cause the creation or storage of fat. This is why it is arguably crucial in battling diabetes and obesity. It is a controversial herb, though, and is still banned for sale as a food or food ingredient in many countries, owing to concern that it could contribute to cancer – although that is much disputed.

Comfrey

―――――――

*With broad, hairy oblong leaves, black turnip-like roots,
and purplish bell-like flowers, comfrey is a speedy-growing
European herb with a dark side.*

GROW
Sow comfrey seeds in pots or trays under glass and transplant them outdoors when the plants are well grown. Comfrey prefers full sun and rich, moist, well-drained soil. It can be invasive, so if you do not want the plants to spread, cut them back when the flowers form.

ITS NICKNAMES – KNITBONE AND BONESET – derive from the herb's Latin name, *Symphytum*, from the Greek *symphis*, for 'bone': comfrey has long been used to heal broken bones and speed up wound healing. Nowadays, this relative of borage (page 51) is very controversial because of its potential to cause liver damage. It should not be taken by mouth or used on broken skin.

Historically, though, comfrey was more than readily used. Alexander the Great was said to have been treated with it. Comfrey baths were commonplace in the Middle Ages. The roots were believed in the seventeenth century to be so sticky that they could bind together chopped meat – a rather bizarre idea today, but one mentioned by Nicholas Culpeper himself. In the mid-1800s the Quaker Henry Doubleday – looking for a postage-stamp glue – heard of comfrey's mucilaginous qualities and grew a large amount of it. It is unclear if he developed it successfully for this reason, but it did end up as animal fodder.

High in potassium, comfrey is no longer eaten by humans or animals, although in the past it has been used as a flavouring herb for homemade wine, and in Bavaria the leaves were eaten fried in batter. Comfrey is more likely to feed your garden than you: its rotted-down leaves can make a vigorous feed for plants. This liquid – the colour of cola – can be diluted and used on tomato plants and, indeed, on anything that needs a helping hand. Warning: you might want a peg for your nose, because it stinks.

Tanacetum balsamita

Alecost

*An extremely popular herb in Europe in the sixteenth century,
alecost was well known for two things: bookmarks and beer.*

GROW
It is possible to grow alecost from seed, but if seeds are difficult to obtain, buy established plants, divide them and plant directly in the garden or in pots. Growing in shade encourages strong leaves. For the best flavour, harvest the leaves before the plant flowers.

EAT WITH
Eggs, seafood, veal, pork, beef, lamb, chicken, salad greens, summer fruit.

TRY
Add a few shredded alecost leaves to stuffings or salads. Use in chilled drinks or fruit salads in place of mint. Stir a little finely snipped alecost into melted butter and toss with boiled new potatoes.

HEAL
Today alecost is most likely to be used in ointments, along with other herbs, to treat sores and itching, or in bathwater for relaxation. A calming potpourri can be made with alecost, rosemary (page 171), cloves, bay (page 106), cinnamon and sage (page 175).

STIFF, LEAFY STALKS bear silver-haired, pale-green leaves and tiny yellow-and-white button-like flowers that give off a pleasant balsamic fragrance. Alecost leaves were once dried and kept inside family Bibles – handy for sniffing to keep awake during long sermons – hence the herb's other name, bible leaf.

Alecost was originally used as a flavouring for ales and spiced wines. It is sometimes called allspice, which may be a variant of ale-spice, or perhaps the scent was felt to be redolent of the better-known sweet allspice berries. Of its other names, sweet tongue refers to the shape of the leaves and their taste, while costmary derives from the herb being dedicated to Mary Magdalene. The mint flavour in alecost is beneficial in the kitchen, although it can be pungent, with a bitter tang, so prepare to use it sparingly. The leaves can also be dried to make a potpourri.

This native of the Mediterranean has a long history: according to the twentieth-century German botanist Heinrich Marzell, it was mentioned in a plant catalogue in AD 812. It was widely grown in herb gardens for its medicinal benefits from medieval times until well into the nineteenth century, and used to treat everything from dysentery to liver ailments and delayed menstruation. Nowadays it is less commonly found in Europe – although it is available from some specialist herb suppliers, of course – but it is still used widely in southwest Asia.

Feverfew

———

The astrological herbalist Nicholas Culpeper linked herbs
to the stars and planets, and feverfew was no exception.

GROW
Plant in April in good, well-drained soil enriched with manure. The plant has a strong, bitter smell, so won't attract bees, but you might get snails or slugs. Dusting the soil with ashes and soot deters the former, while encouraging toads into your garden will help with the latter.

TRY
Add a few feverfew leaves to a green salad dressed with a honey vinaigrette to offset the bitterness.

HEAL
Despite its name, feverfew has never been used for fever. It is renowned for preventing and treating migraines. An infusion can help with period pain. Be careful, though: eating fresh feverfew leaves can cause mouth ulcers, and it should be avoided during pregnancy.

OF IT, HE wrote: 'Venus commands this herb, and has commended it to succour her sisters.' He goes on to prescribe feverfew to women for everything from womb cleansing to 'the disease of the mother', suggesting that a decoction of feverfew flowers be added to wine with a little nutmeg and drunk many times a day to expel the 'dead-birth and after-birth'. Childbirth, of course, was much more of a life-or-death situation in Culpeper's time than it is now, and he went on to write many herbal books specifically for women. Nowadays feverfew is barely used, and in fact it should not be taken by pregnant women, or anyone on anticoagulant medicines, since it may increase the risk of bleeding.

Daisy-like feverfew, also known as wild camomile and bachelor's buttons, has green leaves, torn around the edges. The hard, round stalks bear single flowers consisting of small white petals standing around a central yellow thrum. The scent is strong and the taste bitter: sachets of dried feverfew leaves can make a good moth repellent, while a decoction made from the leaves functions as a basic household disinfectant.

Dandelion

'The dandelion was long popularly known as the "pissabed" because of its supposed diuretic properties, and other names in everyday use included "mare's fart", "naked ladies", "twitch-ballock", "hounds-piss", "open arse", and "bum-towel".'

BILL BRYSON, A SHORT HISTORY OF NEARLY EVERYTHING, 2003

GROW
Dandelions grow freely in gardens and on grassland. You can buy gourmet varieties, such as French dandelion and Arlington dandelion, for variations on bitterness. They tend to be less invasive than the native form, too.

EAT WITH
Beetroot, lettuce, bacon, soft cheese, nuts, pulses, eggs, rice.

TRY
Sauté young dandelion leaves as you would spinach. Add raw young dandelion leaves to a green salad with lardons and a mustardy dressing, topped with a poached egg if you like. Add the petals to a frittata or scatter them over rice dishes as a garnish.

HEAL
A decoction of dandelion can be helpful for osteoarthritis, acne and psoriasis, and to stimulate the liver. An infusion of dandelion leaves can help with high blood pressure. The leaves can be added to juices for their antioxidants, or juiced alone in large quantities.

THE DANDELION IS one of the most useful medicinal plants, being both safe and effective. The roots are a laxative and the leaves a diuretic, and the flowers can be boiled with sugar to treat coughs. The first medicinal use of the dandelion was recorded in the tenth century. Since then, it has been recommended for everything from curing warts to treating liver and kidney problems, and has been known by an entertaining array of common names. The wide range of medicinal uses should come as no surprise, really, given that this herb – often disregarded as a weed – is rich in vitamins A, B, C and D. Indeed, it contains more vitamin A than do carrots.

Not only can the pleasantly bitter leaves and sweet, crunchy flowers be used in cooking, but also the roots can be dried and roasted for dandelion coffee – although to all intents and purposes it is nothing like coffee. Use the leaves sparingly, since they can be bitter; you can put a bucket over them as they grow to blanch them and reduce the bitterness. A dandelion risotto, made with the flower petals, is a visual treat. It is also well worth making your own sweet dandelion wine, but you'll need a good number of blossoms for this.

The name comes from the French *dent de lion* ('lion's tooth'), although the poet herbalist Geoffrey Grigson writes of his incredulity: 'But is there really anything leonine and dental about the leaves?'

Thyme

'I know a bank where the wild thyme blows.'
WILLIAM SHAKESPEARE, A MIDSUMMER NIGHT'S DREAM

GROW
Thyme needs well-drained, sandy soil and as much sun as possible. Pick the leaves regularly to prevent it from becoming woody.

EAT WITH
Poultry, pork, lamb, beef, game, fish, leeks, sweet potatoes, squash, carrots, potatoes, beetroot, celery, celeriac, tomatoes, lentils, beans, cheese, cream, eggs, pasta, chocolate, orange, lemon, apples.

TRY
Add a teaspoon of thyme leaves and a handful of white chocolate chips to lemon muffins or a lemon cake. Decorate with lemon-flavoured glacé icing and a few thyme flowers, if you have any.

HEAL
An infusion of common thyme can ease common colds, hayfever and irritable bowel syndrome. Gargle it if you have a sore throat.

IN THE MIDDLE Ages thyme was put under pillows to aid a good night's sleep, and women gave knights bunches of it to foster courage (the knights tucked it into their clothing or armour as a badge of honour). No wonder thyme was the go-to herb during the Black Death in the 1340s: thymol, the powerful antiseptic found in this herb, is still used today in mouthwashes, soaps and acne ointments.

Woody and straggly, this small, aromatic herb grows wild on the hot, arid hillsides of the Mediterranean basin. There are plenty of kinds of thyme to bring into your life, including pine-scented *Thymus broussonetii*, tangerine-tasting *T. caespititius* and broad-leaved *T. pulegioides*, whose cultivars include oregano. Yet arguably the most pleasing of all is *T. vulgaris*, or ordinary garden thyme, with its wonderful ability to hold its own without overwhelming other ingredients. Perhaps this is why thyme is an essential component of a bouquet garni, along with bay and parsley. Tied together with string and added to casseroles, these herbs withstand long, slow cooking better than most. Thyme is also a classic in stuffings and marinades, where it gently adds flavour but is never strident. As does rosemary, thyme makes a surprisingly good partner for chocolate.

Za'atar is the Arabic name for wild thyme and also the name given to a seasoning made of wild thyme, salt, sumac and sometimes sesame seeds and other herbs. It is sprinkled over dishes for an extra layer of flavour or enjoyed simply by dipping flatbreads into olive oil and then into a small bowl of za'atar.

Thymus citriodorus

Lemon Thyme

For a fresh, lemony note, lemon or citrus thyme is the go-to herb: a lovely addition to any herb garden and useful in the kitchen, too.

A LOW-GROWING, FAIRLY SLOW-GROWING evergreen shrub, lemon thyme is at its most lemony just before it flowers. As with all herbs, it is best to harvest the leaves in the morning, while they are saturated with flavour (the heat of the sun will cause essential oils to vaporize). Lemon thyme offers the best of both worlds to cooks, combining the softness of thyme with the subtlety of lemon, without the bitterness of either.

Lemon thyme's gentle citrus notes make it a must for inserting under the skin of a chicken with plenty of butter before roasting, and also for enhancing fish and seafood. It is one of the best thymes to use in sweet recipes: try it in tarts, biscuits or cookies, creamy desserts and cakes. A few leaves muddled into cocktails work well, and you can decorate the glass with a sprig, too. The herb will give an earthy, herbal kick to homemade lemonade.

The plant is used by herbalists as a tea to treat infections and congestion, thanks to its key constituents: geraniol, esters, citronellol, citral and thymol.

Nettle

This hardy perennial loses its sting once cooked, and is ideal in soup, risotto or even pesto.

GROW
If nettles don't already grow in your garden, go foraging for them, remembering to take gloves with you. Look for new growth in March and April and pick only the tips – the first four or six leaves on each spear. Don't eat them after they have begun to form flowers, from late April, as they will be too tough.

EAT WITH
Rice, soft cheese, eggs, potatoes, garlic, onions, fish, chicken.

TRY
Cook nettles briefly in boiling water, then drain them and squeeze out all the liquid, as for spinach. Add to risotto, buttery mashed potatoes, omelettes or frittata.

HEAL
There is such a thing as urtification, or lashing arthritic joints with stinging nettles; it is painful, but studies show that it can help. Only do it with expert advice. An infusion of stinging nettle can be useful for rheumatism and eczema or as a hair rinse for dandruff. A tincture could help with hayfever.

DESPITE THE RISK of being stung, humans have done all sorts with *Urtica* (its name comes from *uro*, the Latin for 'burn'): nettles have been used to make fabric, a dark-green dye for camouflage and remedies for hair loss and dandruff. In a funny way, stinging nettles love humans: they need phosphates in soil to thrive, so they are keen on our phosphate-rich rubbish dumps and livestock paddocks.

The seventeenth-century herbalist William Salmon suggests that nettles first appeared in England at Romney in Kent, where 'Julius Caesar with his soldiers landed and staid for a time, whence it is thought the place took its name, being by them called Romania.' Apparently, the soldiers would beat themselves with nettles to keep their blood moving in the cold.

Nettles lose their sting within seconds of being added to the cooking pot, and it's worth taking advantage of the many benefits they have to offer as a food. Simply simmer them in a soup or cook them as you would spinach. They beat both spinach and broccoli for vitamin C and iron content. Nettle tea is a natural spring tonic, reputedly good for the heart and for headaches, high blood pressure, skin inflammation and even hayfever.

Valerian

---

*It might smell like dirty socks, but valerian has all sorts of
medicinal benefits, for humans and four-legged creatures alike.*

GROW
The stinky roots like to
be kept cool and damp in
summer, so sow seeds in
any soil that does not dry
out, in sun or partial shade.

HEAL
A cup of valerian-root
decoction before bed can
help with insomnia. A
compress can soothe muscle
cramps. It can be taken
in tea, tincture, capsule or
tablet form for colds, fever,
shortness of breath and
wheezing. Do not take over
a long period of time or if
you are pregnant.

INDIGENOUS TO EUROPE and West Asia, and now at home in
North America too, moderately sized, perennial-flowering valerian is
found in grasslands, ditches and damp meadows. Its sweet-smelling
flowers are light pink or white and it can be readily spotted by its
even, opposing leaves with broad blades. Unusually, valerian's leaves
are asymmetrical both radially and laterally.

Valerian has all kinds of names: tagara, St George's herb,
blessed herb, all-heal, vandal root – and phu (pronounced pooh).
The root reeks when dug up. The herb is an elixir to cats, even more
so than catnip (see page 134): three drops of a decoction of valerian
added to an anxious cat's water bowl should do the trick. Dogs,
horses, rats and mice are all said to find valerian soothing – which is
why legend tells that the Pied Piper of Hamelin carried the root to
entice the rats.

Nicholas Culpeper wrote that valerian was good 'boiled with
liquorice, raisins and aniseed' for the 'short-winded' and those with
coughs, and also for expelling 'wind in the belly'. It was said to be
the valium of the nineteenth century, partly because of its sedative
qualities: it contains a group of ingredients called valepotriates,
which inhibit the breakdown of a natural tranquillizer. Valerian
tea, available in supermarkets, can allegedly improve sleep quality
without causing grogginess.

Vervain

———

*A powerful protector against demons and disease in the
Middle Ages, vervain even featured in a medieval herbal
couplet: 'Vervain and Dill/ hinder witches from their will.'*

GROW
Sow the small seeds indoors
in early spring, and transplant
them outdoors a couple of
weeks after the last frost.
Keep the soil moist.

HEAL
An infusion of vervain can
improve digestion and lower
a fever, and a tincture can
help with stress, anxiety
and depression. As a cream,
vervain can be used on
eczema and wounds.

VERVAIN IS A native perennial of Mediterranean regions,
bearing small, pale lilac flowers. Also known as herb of grace, holy
herb, pigeon's grass and simpler's joy, it is the herb of magic. The
Egyptians believed that it was born from the tears of Isis, goddess
of the dead and of healing; the Romans used it to purify their
altars after sacrifice; the Druids added it to their holy water; and
it has been used by magicians and sorcerers in various rites and
incantations. Bruised, vervain – or wizard's herb – was worn around
the neck as a charm against headaches and snakebites, and for
general good luck. Legend has it that it was used to stop the flow
of Christ's blood at the Crucifixion.

Given the air of magic and suspicion that surrounds vervain,
it is no wonder that the herb is associated with aphrodisiac qualities,
not to mention alleviating suppressed menstruation and other
matters of blood and of passion. It has traditionally been used to
strengthen the nervous system and to treat depression and nervous
exhaustion. As a poultice, it is said to be good for headaches,
rheumatism and piles. A slightly astringent-tasting vervain tea is
made in certain parts of France, and is said to improve sleep, mood
and digestion. Do bear in mind that there has been little or no
research into the effects of vervain on pregnant or breast-feeding
women, so it is recommended that they avoid it.

Heartsease

———

*This beautiful flowering herb has some wonderful
and evocative alternative names.*

GROW
Heatsease self-seeds and grows well in both open soil and pots. Plant in a cool spring, in a position with shade and moisture.

TRY
Use the flowers, either fresh or crystallized, to decorate cakes and desserts. To crystallize them, brush the petals with lightly beaten egg white, sprinkle with caster (superfine) sugar and leave on baking parchment to dry overnight. Geoffrey Grigson recommends tucking heartsease flowers 'in the gully of a book', as the Elizabethans did – making a herbal bookmark that develops a scent as it dries.

HEAL
Added to cough syrups, heartsease can soothe sore throats, colds and bronchitis. Along with other violas, heartsease, mashed up and applied as a poultice, is sometimes used to treat skin problems and thinning hair.

THERE'S LOVE-IN-IDLENESS, LOVE-LIES-BLEEDING, call-me-to-you, kiss-her-in-the-buttery, kiss-me-love-at-the-garden-gate and kiss-me-quick. There's even stepmother (in France and Germany), since the differently coloured petals are said to represent a stepmother, her children and her stepchildren. And then there's johnny-jump-up, monkey's face, three-faces-under-a-hood, two-faces-in-a-hood and cuddle-me.

A wildflower from Europe and North America, heartsease grows on wasteland and in fields and hedgerows. Its beautiful flowers are purple, yellow or white, or more usually a combination of all three. The upper petals are more showy, tending towards purple, while the lower ones are yellower. Although it is related to the violet, heartsease does not produce the cleistogamous (self-pollinating) flowers that violets do. Cleverly, the flower protects itself from rain and dew by drooping its head in wet weather and at night, so that the face is spared excess moisture.

Heartsease flowers are edible – if you can bear to eat something so pretty – and have a mildly sweet taste. Not surprisingly, given its name, the plant has many medicinal applications. With strong anti-inflammatory and diuretic properties, it is often used for gentle stimulation of the circulatory and immune systems.

Everyday Herbarium

Everyday Herbarium

Symptom–Herb Matches

Skin and hair health . . *Marigold, lavender, nettle, thyme*

Digestion . . . . . . *Fennel, peppermint, camomile, meadowsweet, marsh mallow*

Cardiovascular disease . *Nettle, ginger, yarrow, rosemary*

Coughs, colds and flu . . *Garlic, yarrow, echinacea, thyme, sage*

First aid . . . . . . *Marigold, camomile, echinacea*

Muscles and joints. . . *Meadowsweet, rosemary, St John's wort*

Mind and emotions . . *St John's wort, lemon balm, vervain, lavender*

Pregnancy . . . . . *Camomile, lavender, marigold, dill*

Women's health . . . *Lady's mantle, camomile, rose, vervain*

Men's health . . . . . *Ginkgo, ginseng, nettle*

The Symbolism of Herbs

Courage . . . . . . *Basil, chives, nettle*

Health . . . . *Angelica, coriander, poppy seed, camomile*

Peace . . . . *Marjoram, mint, sage, lemon balm*

Travel . . . . *Caraway, dill*

Fertility . . . . . . *Mint, coriander*

Insight . . . . *Lemongrass, marjoram*

Luck . . . . *Comfrey*

Protection . . . . . *Angelica, basil, bay, dill, garlic, mint*

Happiness . . . . . *Feverfew, mint*

Love . . . . *Sorrel, coriander*

Money . . . . *Basil, dill, spearmint, honeysuckle, camomile*

Success . . . . *Bay, lovage, camomile, rosemary*

Herbs for Wellbeing

Rosemary	Echinacea
St John's wort	Ginseng
Garlic	Ginkgo
Holy basil	Camomile
Sage	

Herbs for Beauty

Face mask	*Lavender, calendula*
Face scrub . . . . ,	*Rose, lavender, elderflower, camomile*
Face spritz	*Aloe vera, rosemary, mint, dill, parsley, elderflower*
Foot soak	*Rosehip, bay*
Body rub	*Lavender, rosemary, calendula, camomile*
Body bath.	*Nettle, yarrow, mint, camomile, marigold, mugwort, marjoram*
Hair tonic	*Calendula, comfrey, rosemary, sage, borage, nettle, basil*
Body powder	*Calendula, lavender, sage*

Herb Flavours

Refreshing . . . . . *Parsley, purslane, borage, perilla, mitsuba, orach*

Sweet . . . . *Marigold, basil, bay, angelica, scented geranium, woodruff, lavender*

Zingy . . . . *Lemon balm, sassafras, sorrel, houttuynia, rice paddy herb*

Liquorice . . . . . . *Chervil, tarragon, dill, fennel, anise hyssop*

Minty . . . . *Mint, calamint, catnip*

Oniony . . . . *Garlic, chives*

Bitter . . . . *Celery, lovage, hyssop, chicory*

Spicy . . . . *Oregano, marjoram, rosemary, sage, thyme, savory, micromeria, coriander*

Salady . . . . *Rocket, miner's lettuce, watercress, parsley, fennel*

Herbs for Tisanes

Peppermint   Nettle

Camomile   Elderflower

Lemon balm   Rosemary

Dandelion   Vervain

Rosehip   Houttuynia

Herbs for Cocktails

Basil . . . . *with rhubarb and vodka*

Lavender . . . . . . *with honey, amaretto and silver rum*

Mint . . . . *with strawberry, kiwi and rum*

Elderflower . . . . . *with gin and mint*

Coriander . . . . . *with pineapple, tequila and lime*

Lemon verbena . . . *with gin, soda and lime*

Oregano . . . . . . *with white rum and pineapple*

Thyme . . . . *with blackberry syrup and Prosecco*

Lemongrass . . . . . *with ginger, gin and bitters*

Rosemary . . . . . . *with fig, vodka, lemon and soda*

Herbs for Flavoured Water

Basil . . . . *with strawberry*

Mint . . . . *with blueberries, peach and lemon*

Sage . . . . *with blackberries*

Rosemary . . . . . . *with watermelon*

Mint . . . . *with cucumber and lime*

Lemongrass . . . . . *with cucumber*

Rosemary . . . . . . *with raspberry*

Mint . . . . *with pineapple*

Basil . . . . *with lime*

Herbs for Vegetables

Asparagus	*Dill, marjoram, rosemary*
Beetroot	*Pepper, coriander, thyme, dill, chives, sage*
Broccoli	*Sage, chives, oregano, thyme, rosemary, garlic, marjoram*
Cabbage	*Bay, garlic, marjoram, chives, parsley*
Courgette	*Garlic, basil, parsley, oregano*
Green beans	*Parsley, dill, bay, thyme*
Lettuce	*Basil, chives, thyme, tarragon, dill, parsley*
Mushrooms	*Coriander, basil, garlic, marjoram, sage*
Peas	*Tarragon, mint, parsley, sage, marjoram, basil*
Tomatoes	*Basil, tarragon, chives, dill, mint, oregano, fennel, parsley*

Herbs for Meat

Beef	*Rosemary, basil, savory, chervil, bay, thyme, tarragon*
Lamb	*Thyme, chervil, dill, basil, lemon balm, coriander*
Ham	*Lovage, rosemary, mint, parsley, coriander*
Pork	*Tarragon, oregano, sage, coriander, dill, chervil, fennel*
Veal	*Mint, savory, basil, chervil, thyme, sage*
Turkey	*Parsley, sage, oregano, basil, rosemary, tarragon*
Chicken	*Sage, rosemary, thyme, mint, borage, fennel*

Herbs for Fish

Sea bass	*Marjoram, dill, oregano, thyme*
Catfish	*Oregano, thyme, bay*
Rock bass	*Thyme*
Perch	*Basil, dill, tarragon*
Pike	*Marjoram, parsley, basil, coriander, mint, thyme*
Salmon	*Dill, parsley, tarragon, basil, bay, thyme*
Trout	*Thyme, bay, coriander*
Flounder	*Parsley, coriander*
Haddock	*Thyme, oregano*
Mackerel	*Basil, parsley*
Skate	*Parsley, oregano, thyme*
Shellfish	*Marjoram, thyme, chives, tarragon, bay*

Herbs for Salads

Parsley	Dandelion
Basil	Borage
Lovage	Chervil
Lemon balm	Tarragon
Chicory	Mint

Herb Mixes

Chermoula	Herbes de Provence
Fines herbes	Bouquet garni
Persillade	Farcellets
Gremolata	

Herbs for Everyday Life

Heartsease, alecost . . *for using as a bookmark*

Woodruff . . . . . . *for freshening bookshelves*

Rosemary, lavender . . *for making hair conditioner with coconut oil*

Yarrow, camomile, lavender,
    marigold . . . . . *for making a sitz bath*

Meadowsweet . . . . *for strewing*

Camomile . . . . . *for making a camomile lawn*

Hops . . . . *for making pillows*

Lavender . . . . . . *for making water-based sunburn spray*

Lovage . . . . *for inserting into shoes as foot deodorizer*

Pandan . . . . *for making place mats*

Ways to Keep Herbs Handy

Drying

Freezing

Turning into herb butter

Making herb vinegar

Making herb-flavoured oil

Indoor Herbs

Lemongrass	Oregano
Chives	Thyme
Mint	Rosemary
Parsley	Basil
Rau răm	Garlic

Container Herbs

Mint	Rosemary
Chives	Coriander
Sage	Basil
Bay	Sorrel
Thyme	

Shade-Loving Herbs

Chervil	Comfrey
Parsley	Lemon balm
Coriander	

Sun-Loving Herbs

Rosemary	Parsley
Thyme	Basil
Sage	

Index by Common Name

Select Bibliography

Lesley Bremness, *The Complete Book of Herbs*, Dorling Kindersley, 1988

Colin Clair, *Of Herbs and Spices*, Abelard-Schuman, 1961

Nicholas Culpeper, *Culpeper's English Physician and Complete Herbal*, 1790

Alan Davidson, *The Penguin Companion to Food*, Penguin, 2002

Thomas Fassam, *An Herbarium for the Fair*, Yale University Library Gazette, 1949

John Gerard, *The Herball or Generall Historie of Plantes*, 1636

Patience Gray, *Honey from a Weed*, Prospect Books, 2009

Mrs M. Grieve, *A Modern Herbal*, Jonathan Cape, 1931

Geoffrey Grigson, *A Herbal of All Sorts*, Phoenix House, 1959

C. F. Leyel, *Herbal Delights: Tisanes, Syrups, Confections, Electuaries, Robs, Juleps, Vinegars and Conserves*, Faber, 1937

John Lust, *The Herb Book*, Bantam, 1974

Jekka McVicar, *Jekka's Herb Cookbook*, Random House, 2010

——, *Jekka's Complete Herb Book*, Kyle Books, 2011

Stefano Mancuso and Alessandra Viola, *Brilliant Green: The Surprising History and Science of Plant Intelligence*, Island Press, 2013

Jill Norman, *Herbs & Spices*, Dorling Kindersley, 2002

Claudia Roden, *A New Book of Middle Eastern Food*, Penguin, 1985

William Salmon, *The English Herbal*, 1710

Kay N. Sanecki, *Wild and Garden Herbs*, Transatlantic Arts, 1956

Alice M. Tudor, *A Little Book of Healing Herbs*, The Medici Society, 1927

Acknowledgments

THANKS ARE DUE to many people, each of whom has contributed in different ways to the making of this book.

TO THE TEAM at Thames & Hudson: Lucas Dietrich, Bethany Wright, Andrew Stanley and Rosie Keane, for seeing the possibilities for the world of herbs we had imagined, and for giving us the opportunity to bring our vision to life.

TO JANE MIDDLETON for invaluable advice, help and editorial rigour, along with excellent culinary advice; and to Julie Martin for making the layout happen so smoothly.

TO EVERYONE IN our studio, Here Design, for creating such wonderful imagery with such enthusiasm, especially Ashlea O'Neill, a fabulous designer and illustrator, who took on the gargantuan task of illustrating so many of the herbs.

TO MARK PATON, Kate Marlow and Tess Wicksteed, my partners at Here, who have helped steer this project with such positive enthusiasm.

TO JEKKA McVICAR, 'Queen of Herbs', and her daughter Hannah, for welcoming us so warmly at your beautiful Herb Farm and telling us some of your herb stories.

TO KARA JOHNSON, whose skills in managing this unruly beast, so smoothly and seemingly effortlessly, have kept us all on track from beginning to end.

TO PHILIP COWELL, well, there just couldn't have been a book without you! Thank you for becoming an expert on all things herbaceous, for your fortitude, perfect prose and calming presence.

A word of caution

If foraging, always make sure you know exactly what it is that you are picking. If you have any doubt, don't pick it. Guidebooks to identify edible plants can be helpful or, even better, take someone with you who is experienced in this area. It is your responsibility to be aware of any foraging codes of conduct and relevant legislation that operate in your area.

The information provided in this book is not intended to be construed as or be used as an alternative to medical advice. Speak to your doctor or another healthcare professional before taking any herbs or herbal supplements. The author and publisher cannot be held liable for any health issues that may result from the information presented in this publication.

First published in the United Kingdom in 2016
by Thames & Hudson Ltd, 181A High Holborn,
London WC1V 7QX

Herbarium © 2016 Inkipit Ltd

Designed by Here Design

British Library Cataloguing-in-Publication Data

A catalogue record for this book is available from
the British Library

ISBN 978-0-500-51893-9

Printed and bound in China by C&C Offset
Printing Co. Ltd

To find out about all our publications, please visit
www.thamesandhudson.com. There you can subscribe
to our e-newsletter, browse or download our current
catalogue, and buy any titles that are in print.